CASH RULES

CASH RULES

LEARN & MANAGE

THE 7 CASH-FLOW

DRIVERS FOR YOUR

COMPANY'S SUCCESS

BILL McGUINNESS

KIPLINGER BOOKS
Washington, DC

Published by
The Kiplinger Washington Editors, Inc.
1729 H Street, N.W.
Washington, DC 20006

Library of Congress Cataloging-in-Publication Data

McGuinness, Bill.
    Cash rules : learn and manage the 7 cash-flow drivers for your company's
success / Bill McGuinness.
        p. cm.
    Includes index.
    ISBN 0-938721-75-5 (alk. paper)
    1. Cash flow. 2. Cash management. 3. Accounting. I. Title.

HF5681.C28 M345 2000
658.15'244--dc21   00-048134

This publication is intended to provide guidance in regard to the subject matter
covered. It is sold with the understanding that the author and publisher are not
herein engaged in rendering legal, accounting, tax or other professional services.
If such services are required, professional assistance should be sought.

First edition. Printed in the United States of America.
9 8 7 6 5 4 3 2

Kiplinger publishes books and videos on a wide variety of personal-finance and
business- management subjects. Check our Web site (www.kiplinger.com) for a
complete list of titles, additional information and excerpts. Or write:
    Cindy Greene
    Kiplinger Books & Tapes
    1729 H Street, N.W.
    Washington, DC 20006
    e-mail: cgreene@kiplinger.com
To order, call 800-280-7165; for information about volume discounts, call 202-887-6431.

Acknowledgments

TAKING SOMETHING I KNOW AND CARE ABOUT, IN this case the cash-flow issues underlying almost every business question, and then writing a book about it proved to be a much bigger task than I ever expected. Without the help and encouragement of several key people right from the outset, I may not have seen the job through amid the press of so many other time demands. My heartfelt thanks to those early readers and encouragers: Al Weitlich, my Dad, Ed McGuinness, and most especially my lovely wife—thanks Kath for all your help and patience with the book and with me.

A great source of wisdom who helped greatly in giving the manuscript organization and structure was my agent, Karl Weber, who loves books of all kinds and specializes in business books.

Then came the talented editorial team of Arnold Dolan and Hilary Hindsman, who mercilessly worked me and the book over through several drafts. Last but most important is publisher David Harrison, who carefully oversaw the whole project and always knew when to step in and when to step back. He became, as I guess publishers always do, the final editor and never let me stop thinking about how you, the reader, could best be helped to understand and use the principles of *Cash Rules*.

Many thanks, too, to Heather Waugh for her fine eye for design of the book and cover and to Rosemary Neff for her outstanding word sense.

Table of Contents

Effect • Growth Takes Cash • Breakeven Analysis & Contribution Margin • Sustainable Sales Growth • Big-Gulp Sales Growth & Cash-Flow Implications

Introduction

ASH FLOW IS THE RODNEY DANGERFIELD OF BUSI-
ness management. It never gets the respect it
deserves—that is, until a business runs into trouble paying its bills. Cash is like the air that we
breath: It's taken for granted, but desperately
missed when cut off. And like that other precious commodity,
water, we tend to overuse it when it's plentiful, regretting our
profligacy only when the flow slows to a trickle.

The study of cash-flow management doesn't get its due
these days for one simple reason: The U.S. economy has been
awfully good for an awfully long time. In most major business
sectors, sales have been growing strongly. Credit—both short-
term operating lines and long-term debt—is readily available.
And best of all, investors have been only too eager to throw venture equity at every half-baked idea that comes down the pike.

When business is booming like this, it's no wonder that a lot
of managers and stockholders have become rather blasé about
cash flow. Boom times breed sloppy habits, such as overstaffing
and overspending on everything from marketing to administrative overhead. And, consistent with the old adage that you
never spend someone else's money as carefully as you spend
your own, this overspending is especially flagrant at start-up
firms that are running entirely on outside capital.

To help combat these bad habits, I commend to you this
wonderfully wise and readable new guide to cash-flow management, by business consultant Bill McGuinness. It comes
along at just the right moment in the U.S. business cycle—just
in time to refresh the memories of a lot of older executives
who have lived through both good times and bad times, but

who may have forgotten the latter. More significantly, it should be mandatory reading for every young business manager who may have gotten the impression that cash grows on trees, or bubbles up from the ground, or—more to the point—arrives every payday in the bulging satchels of sugar daddies known as venture capitalists.

Traditionally, new businesses were content to grow at a moderate rate, and this was perfectly acceptable to their financial backers, whether bank lenders or stockholders. A plan of moderate growth gave the new business plenty of time to test its products and services, get to know the market, listen to its customers and find the right people to staff the enterprise. A business plan calling for moderate growth would also conserve cash, giving comfort to lenders and investors. And it would increase the odds of reaching profitability fairly early, albeit at a modest level. If all went well, the new business would prosper over time, gradually winning market share from other firms in the same field.

But the business boom of the 1990s turned these traditional rules upside down. An assumption took hold—mistakenly, I believe—that victory will always be won by the company that hits the market first and fastest with a new concept. The new mantra is "rapid growth at any cost." Cash is something not to be managed but to be spent as quickly as necessary to gain the greatest market share. Another assumption of the New Economy—also mistaken—is that additional rounds of outside capital will always be available to fuel the business, so long as the firm's revenue and market share are growing fast.

As Mr. McGuiness writes in *Cash Rules*, "Growth takes cash, and fast growth takes lots of cash." Old-Economy executives have long been aware of the treacherousness of overly rapid growth. In their long careers, they've seen many potentially successful businesses do themselves in by forcing growth too fast so that product quality or customer service suffered and the cost of over-expansion badly outstripped revenue before more financing could be lined up.

Now it's the New Economy's turn to learn these same time-tested lessons. "Business doesn't run on sales growth; it runs on cash," Mr. McGuiness writes. "Business doesn't run on even the best and most realistic prospects for the future, unless the immediate future contains enough cash to pay your bills."

Bill McGuinness is a passionate apostle of cash-flow management, and he knows of what he speaks. He's got a Harvard MBA, but the lessons he'll teach you include many that he didn't learn in business school. He got on-the-job training in analyzing cash flow when he served as a senior banking executive with Citicorp and Wells Fargo. (Bank lending officers, he notes, had better understand cash flow inside and out if they want to see their loans repaid.) He learned even more as an entrepreneur himself, in three different businesses. As a business consultant and seminar leader, Bill has taught cash-flow management to bankers throughout the U.S. and Canada. And he developed, at Lake Superior (Michigan) State University, one of the first MBA-level courses devoted entirely to cash-flow management.

Here at the Kiplinger publishing organization, we have tried to follow sound practices of cash-flow management throughout the 80 years of our existence as a closely held business. We have been rewarded with decades of steady, if unspectacular, growth in revenue and earnings. But more important, along the way we have earned a reputation for corporate integrity among the people we do business with—our lenders, stockholders, suppliers and subscribers. And we sleep well at night—a benefit not to be slighted in these harrowing times of cutthroat competition. These are the true dividends of sound business management.

On behalf of my colleagues and me, I hope that your business will benefit from the advice in this book, and I wish you the best of success in the challenging years ahead.

Knight Kiplinger

KNIGHT A. KIPLINGER
Editor in Chief
The Kiplinger Letter, kiplingerforecasts.com
and *Kiplinger's Personal Finance* magazine
October 2000

CASH RULES

The ABCs
of Cash Flow

Cash Rules

ASH FLOWS IN AND CASH FLOWS OUT OF EVERY business. Whatever your job, you contribute to both flows: You are a resource that costs dollars, and you use or somehow influence the use of other resources that cost dollars. At the same time, your actions have a direct or indirect effect on cash coming into the business.

But what are the key factors that drive that two-way flow? If you can identify those factors in terms of your company's basic operations, you will gain a powerful tool for growing your business and ensuring that the cash flowing in exceeds the cash flowing out.

This book aims to help you do exactly that. It focuses on what I call *cash drivers,* seven things that control virtually all cash flow for virtually every business almost all of the time. They are: sales growth; gross margins; selling, general and administrative expense (SG&A); accounts receivable; accounts payable; inventory; and capital expenditures (Capex). This book will show you how to understand, measure and analyze your business, as a whole and in its individual parts, in terms of these cash drivers.

You may be the owner or president of the company and trying to come to grips with trade-offs among market share, pricing and profitability. Or maybe sales management is your area, and you need to think through the terms of a new sales-force compensation plan, one that gives adequate attention to a new product line that seems to hold great potential for the company's future. Perhaps you are

Every area of the business, whether product management, sales, purchasing, service or shipping, has issues that can be better managed in light of the dynamics of the seven cash drivers.

responsible for office management and have been asked to hold head-office overhead costs flat as the company expands geographically. Every area of the business, whether product management, sales, purchasing, service or shipping, has issues that can be better managed in light of the dynamics of the seven cash drivers. Before we take a closer look at those cash drivers, though, we need to have a clear sense of the nature and importance of cash flow itself. Let me begin by telling you a story.

Why Cash Flow Is Important

L ast gas for 150 miles." We've all seen that sign in movies, a television show or a cartoon—maybe even in our own travels. My family and I encountered it on a long stretch of highway in central Nevada. Even at 85 and 90 miles per hour, that highway seems to run on forever. The sign looked older than the surrounding desert. Surely the next filling station couldn't be that far away, could it? Why take a chance, I thought while turning in and pulling alongside the $1.99 per gallon self-serve regular pump. A pit stop and something cold to drink sounded good to the whole family, even though the gas gauge registered comfortably in the middle of its range.

An hour and a half later, I had reason to compliment my own forethought. Our older Detroit-built sedan flew past a new 7-series BMW as though it was standing still. Indeed, it *was* standing still. There it sat, svelte and aggressive, $70,000 worth of Bavaria's best iron and engineering ignominiously pulled off to the side of the road. It was, of course, out of gas. The driver had scrawled that painful admission in black crayon on a folded Nevada map he held high, partially unfurled and fluttering in the high-speed turbulence of our well-fueled Oldsmobile. I'm not the sort of person who tends to gloat, but I must admit that I had to mask a pleasant sense of self-righteousness as I stopped to help.

Cash as Fuel

Our friend stranded in the Nevada desert in his $70,000 automobile violated a survival principle: Don't run out of fuel. The overall engineering excellence of the vehicle, the road holding ability of its suspension system, the low coefficient of drag that makes it cut so cleanly through the hot desert air—none of that mattered once the needle pointed to empty. The point is that it is the fuel on board, not the vehicle itself, that is so critical.

When it is fulfilling an economic purpose well, and adapting continuously to its environment, the business can keep on going, like the pink bunny in the battery ad, mostly on internally generated fuel. Companies that aren't so well run are another matter.

Like the expensive import, no matter how glamorous the product, no business can be successful without its fuel—cash—to keep it running. The enterprise that runs out of cash may be the jalopy-like corner grocery store or the long-established Fortune 500 company. Either way, if the enterprise runs out of cash, it is stuck. Every year, thousands of good-sized, first-rate companies go bankrupt, and the core reason is almost always the same. Their managers never learned how to think and plan in cash-flow terms. Consequently, they ran out of fuel.

But like many analogies, this one, too, eventually breaks down. Consider the car. It burns fuel to run, then it must either refuel from an external source or come to a stop. On the other hand, a well-run enterprise has a system that can actually generate much of its own fuel. When it is fulfilling an economic purpose well, and adapting continuously to its environment, the business can keep on going, like the pink bunny in the battery ad, mostly on internally generated fuel. Some proportional increase in bank debt or supplier credit may be part of the fuel-supply system. But these sources of capital are available precisely because of the internal cash-generating capacity of the enterprise.

Companies that aren't so well-run are another matter. You may have a better mousetrap to sell, but if your business cannot generate enough of its own fuel, it will be left by the side of the road. It will probably be cannibalized for parts or transformed into something other than what it was. The business equivalent of running out of gas is bankruptcy, and the company that is unable to pay bills as they come due is at severe risk of being forced into bankruptcy.

Profitability versus Cashflowability

Let's take this point about the self-generation of cash further. The main quantitative measure of a business's success is not profitability—the excess of revenue over expense. Instead, it is what I call cashflowability—the excess of cash flowing into the business over cash flowing out. It is quite possible, and even common, for profitable businesses to be cash-flow disasters. Revenue and expense as the determinants of profitability are accounting notions that very often play out in ways materially separated in time from the actual flows of cash into and out of a company. Sometimes this time warp results in a cash dislocation that can cause serious financial damage.

The most obvious and perhaps most common way for a business to run out of cash is to experience too rapid a rate of sales growth. The CEO of every company needs to know how much sales growth can be handled within given cash constraints. For a simple example, consider a business that has a maximum sustainable sales growth of 25%. Suppose further that this company has a strong new product concept, that its production methods are world class and that its sales efforts are extremely well targeted. In consequence, sales shoot up by 50% rather than 25%. The problem here is that higher speed—more rapid growth—means:

- **higher rates of cash consumption;**
- **less time to regenerate cash supplies; and**
- **greater risk for holders of both debt and equity** (bonds and stocks).

Consider some likely cash impacts of continuing to grow at twice your sustainable rate. Perhaps, through a pattern of slow payment to support a larger inventory, you have already pushed one key supplier to the brink of cutting off all but C.O.D. shipments. You have just missed a payment to the savings and loan holding the mortgage on your new warehouse because so many sales have not yet been converted to cash but instead are sitting in accounts receivable. With all of the production overtime caused by so much sales growth, you have a massive bimonthly payroll due the day after tomorrow that you may not be able to cover. But you are profitable! Your income statement says so. It has been audited and it is absolutely right. You are very profitable, but in terms of cashflowability, your back is to the wall.

Growth takes cash, and lots of growth takes lots of cash. The sad fact is that the majority of failing firms are profitable as they enter bankruptcy. No gas, no go.

Growth takes cash, and lots of growth takes lots of cash. You will see the *why* behind this phenomenon in further detail at several points in this book. The sad fact is that the majority of failing firms are profitable as they enter bankruptcy. No gas, no go. These firms concentrated on burning their fuel efficiently rather than on generating adequate fuel quantities. So instead of being able to keep on going, they found themselves pulled far off to the side of the road and in danger of falling into the bankruptcy ditch. Some may make it back. Many won't. What a shame. For many firms, all the pieces were in place—good people, good ideas, first-rate products, strong customer base, outstanding research and development—except that all those talented people somehow were absent the day the teacher covered cash flow.

Cash Is King

You might think that most of these observations apply to smaller companies that live close to the edge—the kinds of companies for whom survival is a crucial issue, if not the main event. While there is some degree of validity to that view, the real question has to do not with company size but with basic economics. Whatever we do with financial and accounting legerdemain, cash is still king, Cash Rules! Many large-company managers are learning this basic reality in the same down-and-dirty way as the small and midsize firms. Here is why.

The stock market pays far more attention to underlying cash-flow realities than it does to reported accounting earnings. Little by little, corporate managers have finally begun to catch on.

To the surprise of many people, small-company owners and their bankers are not the only ones who follow cash flow. The stock market also pays far more attention to underlying cash-flow realities than it does to reported accounting earnings. Little by little, corporate managers have finally begun to catch on. Many, though, continue to favor earnings over cash flow, a bias that is truly costly. It is costly to stockholders and sometimes to the management teams themselves as more cash-flow–sensitive companies take them over and begin the downsizing.

What Is Cash Flow?

Some of the heaviest fog in the business world settles around the phrase "cash flow". The term is seldom used with precision, and it's even more rarely discussed in a practical, systematic way. I've encountered cash flow as the topic of a specific college or MBA-level course only once, and then it was just a one-hour elective class.

Cash flow is simply the difference between the cash flowing into and out of a business over the course of an accounting period. Since it is a net figure, cash flow is positive when actual receipts exceed actual disbursements. The reverse is obviously true; if cash flowing out exceeds cash flowing in, cash flow is negative. At the most basic level, it really is that simple. Later in this book we'll distinguish among operating cash flows, financing cash flows and investing cash flows. But for the moment, the basic definition will serve. One other important issue at this early stage of understanding cash flow is a distinction based on the basic type of accounting system being used.

Avoiding Distortions—Cash versus Accrual

There are two basic accounting systems: cash-based and accrual-based. In a cash-based accounting system, cash flow is quite easy to measure. The till and the checkbook tell the story because nothing is considered revenue until payment is received and nothing is considered an expense until payment is made. For most businesses, though, a cash-based accounting system is far too simplistic to reflect economic realities.

The accrual-based accounting system presents financial results *as though* all the transactions had already been settled in cash. Cash-based accounting contrasts strongly with that approach by recording only what actually *did* take place in cash terms. Each method distorts what really goes on in the business. The cash-accounting approach misrepresents the underlying business and economic realities of the firm in terms of the flow of value. The accrual method leads people unfamiliar with cash flow to believe that the income statement reveals cash truth when in reality it reveals only *as though* cash truth—as though all transactions had been settled in cash. Let's consider some basic accounting principles and specific examples of how distortions can arise if those principles are violated.

There are two basic accounting systems: cash-based and accrual-based. Each method distorts what really goes on in the business.

One basic principle in accounting requires the recording of revenue when the economic activity that generates it is *substantially completed*. In most cases this happens when the product is shipped or the service rendered. If there is a significant time lag between substantial completion and actual payment, then waiting for actual payment before recording the revenue necessarily introduces a distortion.

A similar distortion would be introduced on the expense side if, for example, inventory is expensed only when the supplier is paid. That would mean the inventory is never recorded as an asset. It would also mean that if the inventory is used in a separate accounting period from the one in which it is paid for, a related basic accounting principle—the matching principle—would also be violated. This principle requires that all of the expenses associated with producing revenue in a period be *recorded* in the financial statements of the *same* time period. From both an accounting and an IRS point of view, cash-basis accounting is permissible *only* in businesses that are so simple that cash accounting would not distort results.

Accrual-based accounting measures the flow of *value*, not the flow of cash. But the flow of *cash* and the flow of *value* are quite different in several respects. It is crucial to get behind the details of accrual accounting to understand what happened in cash terms.

In the vast majority of businesses, accrual-based accounting has been adopted as the required method. And this is the point at which problems of terminology and understanding about cash flow begin. Instead of recording everything based on the movement or flow of cash, as in cash-basis accounting, accrual-based accounting measures the flow of *value*. But the flow of *cash* and the flow of *value* are quite different in several material respects. It is crucial, therefore, to get behind the details of accrual accounting to understand what happened in cash terms.

Cash Flow & Credit

Bankers usually understand cash flow better than anyone else. The reason is simple. Bankers are unique in that after they sell you their product—money—they want you to give it back! Loans are made in cash, and lenders insist on being repaid in cash. A good lender, therefore, must understand what it takes for a business's cash flow to be adequate to repay debt as scheduled. The concern is not just repayment, but repayment *as scheduled*—that is, *on time*. And there lies the essence of the cash-flow rub—timing. The bank faces more than just its stockholders on this issue of repayment *as scheduled*. It is also responsible to powerful state or federal regulators who watch for loans not performing as scheduled.

It makes sense that understanding cash flow is at the very core of the banker's business. This has been my personal experience working as a banker and teaching cash-flow dynamics to bankers. The goal is always to help them focus more clearly on their clients' cash-flow potential. I have also been on the other side of the desk as an entrepreneur experiencing the dark side of the cash-flow force when sales volume didn't meet goals, expenses exceeded budget and capital requirements ran beyond plan. I have struggled to cover payables in a start-up enterprise and counseled with clients in similar straits. Believe me when I say, *Cash Rules*.

Whenever it comes time to calculate the total value of a company, the flow of cash will be much more critical than the flow of value that conventional accrual-accounting systems track.

You might think that borrowers would care about and understand their cash flow at least as well as their bankers did, but that's rarely the case. Especially in small- and medium-size firms, businesspeople typically concentrate on satisfying some marketplace demand. They are generally much less adept at support functions such as accounting or finance. If you're running a software company or flower shop, or if you are a plumbing contractor, you probably went into business because you know and care about computer programming, roses or water heaters—not finance, important though it is.

There are plenty of specialists in finance and accounting on whom you might depend. Unfortunately, their experiences and worldviews are shaped primarily by the use of accounting to track the flow of value, not cash—that is, they are primarily oriented to the assumptions that underlie accrual accounting systems. The entire accounting cycle of entries and records, of journals and ledgers, of trial balances and financial statements, is focused on keeping track of the bills we send and the bills we receive—not on the cash that actually pays those bills.

Cash-Based Valuations

The funny thing is that whenever it comes time to calculate the total value of a company, the flow of cash will be much more critical than the flow of value that conventional accrual-accounting systems track. Whether your firm is small or large, public or private is not at issue. In every case, the underlying value of the business will always be subject in some way to a valuation procedure. Someday your business will undergo a valuation process for some purpose—maybe for estate or other tax reasons, perhaps for sale or merger purposes, or (though hopefully not) for divorce or bankruptcy reasons. Whether it is the stock market, the courts, your heirs or a prospective purchaser triggering the valuation, the core of the valuation process will always be rooted in one central issue: the capability of your business to generate a flow of cash into the indefinite future. The greater that flow and the lower the risk *to* the flow, and the higher the growth rate *of* the flow, the greater will be the flow's present value—and the worth of your business.

Turnaround specialist David Allen likens cash to blood. You need enough to stay alive, as he has told many a struggling executive. Blood may be a bit more dramatic than gasoline, but blood, when looked at functionally, is simply a kind of fuel. When a cash crunch pushes a business hard up against the rocks and it is bleeding profusely, it's in a life-threatening situation but not necessarily terminal. Far too often, though, bankruptcy *does* mean the death of the business because three out of four business bankruptcies are the Chapter 7 kind—the kind that means liquidation. Even that word—*liquidation*—carries the root idea of taking something that was not flowing and forcing it to flow. We *liquidate* a business when it is not producing positive cash flow on its own and has little prospect of doing so. Too often this happens *not* because of anything fundamental to the business or its management style. It happens instead due to ignorance of cash-flow realities and dynamics.

Team Cash Flow

Imagine a basketball team composed of outstanding players at every position. For some strange reason, though, the players all suffer from the same defect—a poor understanding of the basic rules of the game. The players may be great at dribbling, passing, shooting and rebounding, but if they don't know that they have to inbound the ball within five seconds, they'll have a hard time beating even vastly inferior opponents, let alone winning the state championship.

Much of every game's success comes from thinking a few moves ahead—that is, knowing what to do next. Good decisions can be made only in the context of a broad understanding of the rules as they affect all the players you might need to cooperate with. In much the same way, knowledge of cash-flow dynamics should be a qualification for virtually any responsible job in your organization. This doesn't mean that you need a company full of accountants, but you do want each key player to see and understand the cash-flow issues clearly. Each one should have a definite awareness of how his or her personal effectiveness and efficiency affect your company's cash flow. Accomplishing this goal involves some basic education and training, as does any new discipline. The purpose of this book is to help you move in that direction—toward making the cash-flow mindset an integral part of your business's operation.

Knowledge of cash-flow dynamics should be a qualification for virtually any responsible job in your organization. This doesn't mean that you need a company full of accountants, but you do want each key player to see and understand the cash-flow issues clearly.

Many small- and medium-size organizations think they cannot afford a trained and experienced chief financial officer. In fact, they cannot afford *not* to have that kind of expertise. But even among those companies that *do* have skilled CFOs, there is no guarantee that the cash-flow way of thinking will get integrated into the organization. The fact is that everybody on your management team needs to understand how cash-flow dynamics affect his or her department if your business is to prosper in the long term. This book is intended not to turn owners or managers into accountants, but to provide you with a set of essential cash-flow insights and a language for dealing successfully with cash-flow dynamics.

If you are in sales, you affect company operations—and thus cash flow—differently than if you are a purchasing agent, a production engineer or a service department manager. If you are a computer programmer, your sphere of influence includes things that the accounts-receivable clerk's job does not. As you work through *Cash Rules*, perhaps as part of a taskforce in concert with others in the company, look for the elements, connections, influences and potentials in your job that may positively affect cash flow either directly or indirectly through the seven cash drivers. The main purpose of this book is to help you integrate cash-flow thinking into both the everyday and the strategic decision-making processes of your company.

Plan of the Book

L et's look now at an overview of the book to see how it can help you develop that most basic of business survival and success skills, cashflowability.

PART ONE: THE ABCS OF CASH FLOW. Following this introductory chapter, we discuss the language and concepts behind cash-flow thinking, including a preliminary sketch of each of the cash drivers and how it is measured. Chapter 3 explains a few of the basic accounting concepts and mechanics you will need to apply the cash drivers to your business. Finally, Chapter 4 focuses on the structuring of cash-flow statements and their relationship to balance sheets and the income statement. The chapter includes a discussion of the relationship between cash flow and more traditional ratios analysis in terms of profitability, efficiency, liquidity and leverage.

PART TWO: THE SEVEN CASH DRIVERS. The drivers appear in descending order of importance to your business. Sales growth is the lead-off driver, both because of its typically greater significance and because of some specialized topics affecting sales growth that warrant special attention before moving on to consideration of gross margin.

Gross margin, the subject of Chapter 6, is what remains after deducting the cost of production, cost of product acquisition or cost of sales from total revenue. It has both a cost side and a price side, and both will be discussed in depth from a cash-flow viewpoint.

Chapter 7 looks at ways of controlling operating expense, that is, selling, general and administrative, or SG&A. The focus is on both expense and expenditure, which are considered from two key perspectives, cost control and capacity planning. Chapters 8, 9 and 10 look in turn at accounts receivable from customers, the inventory we hold for either sale or further work, and, last among so-called working-capital items, accounts payable to our suppliers. We explore both the short- and long-term implications for cash flow in how these three issues are managed. In Chapter 11, long-term investments made for purposes of enhancing productivity under the heading of capital expenditures are examined from a financing, timing and strategic perspective, with emphasis throughout on the cash-flow dimensions.

PART THREE: CASH FLOW AND BUSINESS MANAGEMENT. This section consists of four forward-looking chapters that use the seven cash drivers as the basis for describing, testing and fine-tuning plans for growing your business. Chapter 12 follows up with a nuts-and-bolts case study demonstrating the logical application and calculation of the cash drivers. It does this for both a sample company's recent history and a projection of its near-term future. The projected values of the cash drivers are used to teach a method for building the forecasted periods' cash-flow statements. Chapter 13 goes beyond the cash-driver assumptions and the mechanics of projecting by taking a more strategic perspective. The point of this chapter is to think about the business using the cash drivers as a strategically consistent set of measurable business goals centered in cash-flow dynamics.

Chapter 14 moves to the important link between cash flow and company value. This view begins with a look at the risk levels borne by both your lenders and your stockholders. Regardless of whether these are major institutions or just the friends, relatives and co-workers who gather at the annual picnic, the specific risks to be considered under valuation are always those associated with market-value erosion. Operational risks, of course, are implicitly covered in the discussions of cash drivers. Company valuation is then discussed in the context of a cash-low calculation methodology, with particular attention to the risk of loss. Such risk may be to holders of either debt or equity. The methodology of valuation presented is consistently cash-flow centered, as are the related risks of loss, volatility and inadequate growth. Chapter 15 provides a brief summary of key concepts along with some suggestions for beginning to integrate the cash-drivers mindset into your business life. Now let's begin with an overview of cash flow.

Cash-Flow Language
& Environment

ASH IS THE ULTIMATE MEASURE IN BUSINESS. Acquisitions, expansions, buyouts and bankruptcies all revolve around and depend on measures and flows of cash. Too little cash can kill a business; too much can invite unwanted takeovers. Every significant decision in a business has definite cash impacts and implications, but ironically, there is no generally accepted way to communicate clearly, consistently and simply about this important topic on anything but a detailed accounting basis. Let's begin to remedy that problem by talking a bit more about what cash is and where it comes from.

By cash we mean more than the currency in our wallets and tills. More significant by far are immediately accessible deposit accounts, money-market funds and the instruments, primarily checks, that draw on those accounts as cash. There is also a category of investments that can become cash almost instantly, such as Treasury bills and certificates of deposit. Added together, these make up the *actual cash* figure on the balance sheet of an enterprise.

Economists talk about *money supply* quite a bit and define it in a number of ways that have parallels with different parts of a business firm's *actual cash*. Just as an economy has a money supply, so does a company. For whole economies as well as for individual firms, there is a relationship between the money supply and the velocity, or turnover rate, of that money supply. For a whole economy, the value of everything that gets produced has to be equal to the available money supply times its velocity. The velocity of money in the whole economy is fairly constant and changes very slowly over time in response to a variety of influences. In contrast with the quite slow changes in money's velocity, the money supply itself can change more quickly. Even so, only relatively small percentage changes occur in the money supply over the course of a typical year. When we measure what happens to money supply spontaneously through the loan-expansion or -contraction capacity of the banking system in order to accommodate rising or falling levels of business activity, the change may be a bit higher. Even then, however, money-supply changes are usually measured only in the range of fractions of a percent per month.

Money supply and velocity within a company are both extremely sensitive to market influences and management decision making. As a result, they can change enormously in the very short term. Generally speaking, the money supply and its velocity will have more variability for a smaller company than for a larger one.

In the individual business, things move much more quickly. Money supply and velocity within a company are both extremely sensitive to market influences and management decisions. As a result, they can change enormously in the very short term. Generally speaking, the money supply and its velocity will have more variability for a smaller company and less variability for a larger one. General Motors' balance-sheet figure for cash and cash equivalents, the company's own money supply, will vary far less over the course of a year than will that of the Smith Construction Co. The reason is the law of large numbers. One consequence is that the risk of the money supply's dipping to the danger point is much greater for small enterprises than for large ones. The other element of risk that is related to size is access to capital. Because risk is greater in a small enterprise, it's much harder to get outsiders to plug a gap in the money supply. The good news though, is that the basic categories of available money resupply are the same for all. Let's consider the possibilities.

Under certain conditions and within certain limits, more cash can be generated by converting a variety of other assets to cash, by borrowing, or by taking in cash from investors. There are, however, a whole series of risks, costs, delays and limits to each of these strategies. For example, raising equity funds when the company is strapped to begin with may prove unduly costly if too much equity has to be given up in return.

Under certain conditions and within certain limits, more cash can be generated by converting a variety of other assets to cash, by borrowing, or by taking in cash from investors. There are, however, a whole series of risks, costs, delays and limits to each of these strategies.

Asset conversion is always a possibility for generating cash, and there are two basic ways to accomplish it. The first is to sell off assets that are not essential to the business's operation. The second involves better management and tighter forecasting of the so-called asset-conversion cycle—the sequence during which a sale converts a portion of inventory to a customer receivable, and then eventually to cash as the customer pays. This asset-conversion cycle is fairly regular. A regular cycle, however, doesn't necessarily mean an even one. Lumps and bulges occur due to uneven ordering dates, variations in invoice size, seasonal factors and other reasons that leave the shape of the asset-conversion cycle far from a perfect circle. It often looks more like a prehistoric engineer's attempt at building a wheel by tying a bunch of rocks together. There are lots of irregularities.

The consequences of mismanaging or misestimating these cycles can be dangerous. This is true even for solid businesses, because running out of cash and not having enough time to replenish the money supply leave the firm unable to pay debts as they come due. Obviously, that exposes the company to potential legal action by creditors. It is also dangerous because, even in the absence of legal action, the risk to payroll integrity and supplier confidence may easily cause irreparable damage to the overall quality of the operation. You must, therefore, put the highest priority on paying debts as they come due.

With very few exceptions, debts have to be paid in *cash* as defined above. Salaries have to be paid in cash. Virtually everything has to be paid for in cash. You may get two weeks, or 30 days, or other terms on which payment is due, of course, but when it's due, it's due in cash. When your enterprise has a bill to pay, nobody really wants your delivery truck, or the products sitting in your warehouse, or all the wondrous things your designers, architects or programmers could do for them. Nor does anyone want to be paid with a stack of receivables due, even from your very best customers.

Business doesn't run on profit; it runs on cash. Business doesn't run on sales growth; it runs on cash. Business doesn't run on even the best and most realistic prospects for the future unless the immediate future contains enough cash to pay your bills.

Everyone you owe wants cash. If you can't provide cash when it's due, or somehow reassure your creditors that it's coming very soon, they will most likely force you into bankruptcy. But wait a minute, you say, you're a very profitable business with wonderful prospects, a new product line and a world-class customer base. You have a lock on the market and are growing 40% a year. The answer will simply be: Sorry, payment needs to be made in cash. Business doesn't run on profit; it runs on cash. Business doesn't run on sales growth; it runs on cash. Your business doesn't run on even the best and most realistic prospects for the future unless the immediate future contains enough cash to pay your bills. Cash is the fuel on which the enterprise runs, and we need a language to help us talk simply and consistently about it.

Introducing the Cash Drivers: A New Language

Imagine an environment in which key employees in all kinds of jobs learn to use a simple, cash-focused vocabulary as the primary way of framing business issues and taking part in business discussions. Imagine the improvement in clarity of communications. Imagine the sharpened focus on measurable goals. Imagine the improvement in cash flow and, ultimately, company value. The benefits cross all boundaries. Large firms and small ones, without regard to location, division or product specialty, would benefit. Imagine the possibilities in your company, on your job, if the effects of not only the big decisions but also the relatively ordinary ones were routinely processed through a cash-flow mindset and discussed in common terms. This language consists of the dynamic vocabulary of the seven cash drivers (that I'll detail in Chapters 5 through 11) operating within a basic accounting grammar that I will cover in Chapters 3 and 4. With the background of our basic cash-flow discussions thus far, let's turn to an overview of the cash drivers.

> **Imagine the possibilities in your company, on your job, if the effects of not only the big decisions, but also the relatively ordinary ones were routinely processed through a cash-flow mind-set and discussed in common terms.**

CASH DRIVER #1: SALES GROWTH. The most basic cash driver is the sales-growth rate—typically measured as the percentage change in sale volume from the previous period. Sales growth is one of the first things that lenders, managers and professional financial analysts look at when evaluating business performance. The reason is straightforward: Sales volume tends to drive practically everything else. Other things being equal, significant changes in sales volume will have major ripple effects through the company's balance sheet, income statement and, especially, its cash-flow statement.

CASH DRIVER #2: GROSS MARGIN. Gross margin is what remains from sales after you have covered your direct product or service costs. Gross margin is measured and expressed as a percent of sales to help demonstrate more clearly how many cents out of each sales dollar are available to pay for everything else in the business. All operating, financing and tax costs as well as any return to owners of the business will come out of the gross margin.

CASH DRIVER #3: SELLING, GENERAL & ADMINISTRATIVE EXPENSE (SG&A). This is commonly thought of as your overhead in manufacturing and merchandising businesses. In a service business, where there is often no gross margin per se, SG&A also includes those costs associated with providing the service that is your reason for being. SG&A is generally best expressed as a percent of sales to reveal directly how many cents out of each sales dollar are taken by normal operating expenses.

CASH DRIVERS #4, 5 AND 6: ACCOUNTS RECEIVABLE, ACCOUNTS PAYABLE, AND INVENTORY. Rather than thinking about each of these items as a percentage of sales, as with the preceding drivers, we normally find it most helpful to think about these trading accounts in relation to time. The term is *days' worth*— so many days' worth of annual sales tied up in accounts receivable from your customers, so many days' worth of annual cost of goods sold expenses tied up in your inventory investment, so many days' worth of annual cost of goods sold financed by your suppliers through accounts payable. These *days* measures also have the benefit of simultaneously telling how long it typically takes for three important things to happen: How long it takes to collect on a sale (accounts-receivable days), how long the average item sits in inventory before sale (inventory days) and how long we typically have benefit of a supplier's product or service before actually paying for it (accounts-payable days).

CASH DRIVER #7: CAPITAL EXPENDITURES. What does it take in the way of new investment in the infrastructure of your business to keep it healthy and growing? That's the capital expenditures (Capex) issue. It is usually helpful to measure this cash driver both in absolute terms—that is, in dollars—and also in relative terms linking it to sales growth. The best relative measure I have found is capital-expenditure dollars expressed as a percent of the dollar growth in sales during the same period. It takes more in the way of fixed assets to support higher levels of sales, and so we want to express that reality in a relational way.

If somehow we could know the relative levels of the seven cash drivers for any good sample of companies, say the

Fortune 500, for the coming year, we could predict with amazing accuracy their likely levels of cash flow. Although there are lots of other factors besides these seven, *these are the drivers,* and they are the drivers because imbedded within them are the core issues and relationships of the enterprise. As we focus on each of the drivers in their individual chapters, we will look specifically at what those issues are.

In the small enterprise with perhaps just a handful of employees and sales of up to a few million dollars, the draw that the owners take may reasonably be considered an eighth cash driver.

The cash drivers apply not just to large companies but to *all* organizations, especially businesses, of virtually any size. In the small enterprise with a handful of employees and sales of up to a few million dollars, the draw that the owners take may reasonably be considered an eighth cash driver. That account can vary significantly and, in a sense, represents a special subcategory of SG&A expense. We won't be dealing with this element specifically, but keep it in mind if your situation makes it appropriate.

Some specialized industries may also have their own key measures that can effectively be used as cash drivers—for example, percentage of seats sold (load factor) for an airline, or percentage of homes penetrated on a line for a cable-TV operator. For most of us most of the time, however, the basic seven cash drivers are the appropriate tools. Let's take a mini case study to illustrate some of the areas in which cash-driver language can make business smoother and simpler.

Cash Flow in a Company Context

Imagine that last year you started a company with $5 million you won in the lottery. You have a great product idea: organic memory membranes for use in electronic games. You have hired a few outstanding engineers to implement your brainstorm, and, little by little, you have added other specialists as needed.

Your company's first nine months were spent on design

and development of production equipment, while you and your sales staff negotiated a deal with CyberFun, the world's leading maker of computer games. CyberFun plans to use your memory membranes in its newest line of hand-held toys, to be launched in time for next Christmas. Three months ago, you began shipping your product, in small batches at first, then in progressively larger shipments as your manufacturing yield and product quality improved. There were a few setbacks, of course, and some of the early batches failed to meet the procurement contract specs, but last month's shipment was near-perfect. You can expect a big check from CyberFun by the first of next month. You'll finish Year One with a solid $10 million in sales. It's a huge success story! Or is it?

The seven cash drivers can help you think about what drives cash and focus your attention on the critical issues. They provide an essential paradigm not only for business survival, but for strategy and success.

The problem is that every cent of your $10 million in sales is tied up in a single account receivable from CyberFun. Meanwhile, you've spent all your original $5million (your lottery winnings, remember?) plus $2 million more that you borrowed from your neighborhood banker, Debby at First InterGalactic BanCorp. The first loan repayment is due tomorrow, and you'll have barely enough cash left to meet Friday's payroll. *But your balance sheet and income statement look great!* What happened?

Your balance sheet and income statement reflect a flow of $10 million in product value to CyberFun. The balance sheet shows a $10 million flow of value to you in the form of an account receivable from a first-class, blue-chip company. The income statement calls that $10 million sales, though not a penny has actually changed hands, and shows actual expenses of only $5 million and a $2 million after-tax profit. Yet despite all of that accounting profit, you are out of cash because of the big investments made for carrying receivables and inventory, plus building a state-of-the-art manufacturing facility.

Accrual accounting systems, you will recall, track the flow of value, and they do that very well. But except in the simplest cash businesses, there are inevitably significant differences between the cash flow and the value flow. The seven cash drivers can help you think about what drives cash and focus your attention on the critical issues. They provide an essential paradigm not only for business survival but also for strategy and success. Understanding that paradigm will enable you to contribute more fully to the success of your organization, regardless of your job. Each of the cash drivers is crucial. If you understand what they mean and how to manage them, you will have taken a big step toward ensuring the long-term health of your company. Let's look at a heavily disguised, yet real, company where cash-flow thinking was added on rather than built-in.

A CASE STUDY
Recovering But Still Not a Team

The Jones Dynamite Co. is a medium-size wholesaler of explosives in the Southeast. In the early '90s, there was considerable sales growth because of a successful strategy of renting specialized explosives-related equipment bundled together with the explosives themselves. At the same time, however, a lack of tight controls permitted Jones's overhead expenses to drift upward somewhat faster than sales, thus increasing SG&A expense as a percentage of sales.

But that's not all. While it was concentrating on expanding market share, the company did not pay enough attention to customer credit and collection issues. This allowed dollars that were tied up in accounts receivable to increase even faster than sales grew. From 1991 to 1994, Jones went from holding an average of approximately 35 days' worth of sales in accounts receivable to nearly 50 days. Thus Jones not only had to finance the additional investment in accounts receivable that inevitably comes with rapid sales growth; it also had to finance the excess accounts receivable associated with not paying close enough attention to collection and credit practices. This combination of circumstances used quite a bit of cash over and above what was needed to develop the specialized-equipment rental side of the company's business and to hold larger explosives inventory.

Because of the magnitude of these cumulative cash drains, Jones could easily have become another of the many basically sound companies that fail at the rate of more than one every hour, with no time-out for weekends or holidays. If Jones had failed and filed for bankruptcy, it would not be because the company ran out of energy, good marketing ideas or a broad customer base.

Surprising as it may seem, chances are that most business bankruptcies could be headed off without radical surgery if enough cash was available to keep going just a few months longer—just enough time to solve the new-product bugs, or to absorb the loss of a major client, or to sublet half of that big warehouse, or any number of other problem-solution combinations.

Ignorance of cash-flow dynamics kills more companies than fraud, fire, competition, technological obsolescence or anything else.

The good news is that with the help of their banker and lawyer, the two brothers who own Jones understood that the organization had gotten too big and too complex for their longtime bookkeeper. She had almost no formal training and had come to the company right out of high school as its first full-time office worker. That was ten years after the two owners' father had founded the company on a shoestring following the Korean War. Jones had long ago passed the stage where it should have hired a controller. Many CPAs agree that when a company passes a half-million dollars in sales, a hundred customers and dozens of suppliers, as Jones did in the mid '80s, it should hire a chief accounting officer. And especially in view of the ambitious growth rate in sales that Jones targeted, professional cash-flow planning was a management necessity.

Jones may sound like an extreme example, but it followed an amazingly common pattern. Ignorance of cash-flow dynamics kills more companies than fraud, fire, competition, technological obsolescence or anything else. There are few circumstances that can't be handled and recovered from if key executives and managers have internalized a cash-flow mindset and integrated it into their management style. At Jones, an experienced and professionally trained controller was finally brought in with excellent support from the bookkeeper. Some major improvements were made and some financial discipline was imposed. Much of this discipline was a natural byproduct of the controller's focus on the development and implementation of accounting systems and controls. Another dimension of the job that quite naturally helped was a new emphasis on financial reporting with a view toward identifying implications for the future.

Building a Cash-Flow Culture

J ones has now recovered fully from its near-disastrous cash-flow bind, and yet a major difficulty remains. As is the case with so many organizations, the new financial discipline is essentially being imposed by the controller from a point of view that is conceptually external to the essence of Jones's business. The controller just isn't a construction guy, much less an explosives guy. The people in the company who really know the products, the customers and the specific business environment still don't understand or think about cash flow. They just react to the controller as a sort of cash-flow cop. Even the owners joke publicly about the new financial discipline as though it represents an uncomfortable straitjacket binding the company, rather than something integral and organic to their overall decision-making processes.

There are few circumstances that can't be handled and recovered from if key executives and managers have internalized a cash-flow mindset and integrated it into their management style.

What is missing at Jones is a cash-flow awareness from within instead of a discipline imposed from above. What is needed is a self-discipline that comes from having the cash-flow way of thinking and cash-driver language instilled into every key player on the team.

To some degree, a cultural shift has to take place. Language, which is always basic to any culture, needs to be adjusted to express the new cash-flow realities. To the extent that information and training about cash flow become part of the way people communicate and motivate, then, and only then, is the cultural shift truly under way.

As we think about culture shift, consider a real-life example— the Hudson's Bay Co., the largest department-store chain in Canada. At more than 300 years of age, this former fur-trapping firm might be expected to know something about the importance of survival and cash flow. But just surviving this long proves very little. At one time, albeit a very long time ago, Hudson's Bay was arguably the largest and most prosperous firm in the New World. But if we had the records to calculate its true rate of return over the past three centuries, we would no doubt find that despite the

Bay's size, actual return on investment has been significantly negative on an inflation-adjusted basis.

And recent performance indicates that the company's management still seems to have an inadequate understanding of cash flow. After spending a bundle to acquire Kmart of Canada, the company had little cash left for the major remodeling its aging stores required to appeal to today's fashion consumers. These buyers are critically attuned to their total shopping environment and experience. The Bay must also deal with the cash implications of keener competition in electronics, appliances and other product lines taken over by giant, low-margin specialty retailers. The implications affect not only price but also inventory risk. What's a company to do?

One response has been to beef up customer service at the retail-sales level. It may be too little too late, but at least the company is trying. One element of the plan is somewhat hit or miss, but it is moving in the right direction: The company is rewarding good service on the retail-sales floor, as identified by mystery shoppers, with cash bonuses.

Your company may not have the age or the size or the problems of the Bay, but the simplicity of immediate cash is still a well-understood concept at the most basic level of employment. Those cash bonuses reinforce a simple truth: Better customer service generates more cash, and the company is willing to share some of that cash with deserving employees. Let's now take a more systematic view of the relationship between cash flow and motivational systems.

Goals and Rewards

Bonuses, rewards, commissions and other compensation-plan elements have long been tied to traditional targets such as sales volume and output levels. Once the cultural shift to cash-flow thinking and cash-driver language begins to take hold, the next step is to begin setting cash-flow goals at the level of each significant organizational unit or individual in the company—and then to fully link the goals to the compensation system. People tend to produce what they are measured on and compensated for. As the cash-driver mindset begins to capture and redirect some of your thinking in the course of reading this book, keep in mind this motivational aspect.

In organizations of all sizes, the cash-flow motivational shift is on. In 1998, Pepsico introduced a change for senior division-level managers whose long-term compensation had previously been tied to profit. Under the new plan, the compensation linkage is tied more directly to three-year cash-flow targets in their divisions. The purpose in Pepsi's case isn't a survival issue, as it might be with smaller companies. Rather, it is the conviction that shareholder value is really much more closely related to cash flow than to earnings. Entrepreneurs often understand this at a gut level, but they aren't always very good at tracking it and living by it. Corporate-management people may not have that entrepreneurial gut instinct about cash flow that comes from concern for the company's survival, but they learn really quickly when the survival of their bonus is suddenly at stake.

Once the cultural shift to cash-flow thinking and cash-driver language begins to take hold, the next step is to begin setting cash-flow goals at the level of each significant organizational unit or individual in the company—and then to fully link the goals to the compensation system.

The fact that a large conglomerate like Pepsico has shifted the compensation plan of division managers to reflect cash flow may not *seem* particularly relevant if your firm is a small one, but here is why it is: The Pepsi division manager has the best shot at making her numbers when she has learned how to get every key manager up and down the line to think in cash-flow terms. If those managers are effective, they pass that cash-flow mindset on throughout the organization. At some point, this could mean that there is a bonus for the accounts-receivable clerks responsible for following up on past-due invoices from bottlers. Getting those accounts receivable down by just one day's worth from the division average might be worth 1.5% extra in next month's paycheck. Keep it down for three consecutive months and there could be an additional 1.5% quarterly bonus. That's a cumulative 6% raise for the quarter—maybe enough for the first and last month's lease payment on the new car. The cultural transformation made possible by combining new language with new incentive and goal-setting systems can create real value for shareholders at Pepsico, and it can do the same for your ownership group.

The shift toward cash-flow–based goals and incentive systems isn't just some faddish management technique. It is based on a major new understanding of company value that is permeating corporate America—a recognition that cash-flow management, throughout the organization, is linked even more closely to shareholder value than earnings are. The reasons have to do with issues that relate more to capital allocation and management motivation systems than to mere survival. When those corporate concerns are applied to smaller firms, they may be even more relevant because of the greater scarcity of capital and the greater risks inherent in the smaller business.

> **The shift toward cash-flow based goals and incentive systems isn't just some faddish management technique. It is based on a new understanding of company value that is permeating corporate America—a recognition that cash-flow management, throughout the organization, is linked even more closely to shareholder value than earnings are.**

Ideally, if your people are given a basic education about the significance of the cash drivers—and if those cash-driver terms are integrated into the language of your internal communications—things will begin to change. And as they do, more adaptation to cash-flow thinking becomes possible. Important documents such as job descriptions and performance reviews can be tied to the cash-driver model. Desired results come to pass as cash begins to flow more freely and rapidly instead of pooling and eddying in stagnant pockets, tributaries and backwaters. The final piece in the cultural transformation that your new cash-driver language creates falls into place when your company begins to create appropriate reward systems tied to cash-driver goals.

This chapter has introduced you to the basic vocabulary of cash-driver language, using several case studies to illustrate various points. The hypothetical CyberFun Co. provided a backdrop for seeing more clearly the difference between accrual realities and cash-flow realities. Jones Dynamite continued to develop some of those points and added the relational dynamic of how better financial management rescued the company without really shifting its culture with regard to cash flow. At the Hudson's Bay Co. there was a hint of some culture shift, and at Pepsico there was a clear and forceful move into a strongly cash-flow–oriented management culture.

Before going further in the development of your understanding of cash flow and how it is basically set by your management of the cash drivers, it is important for you to understand the basic context, or grammar, in which cash-driver language functions. That context is accounting, the sometimes dreaded *A* word, and in the next two chapters I will try to minimize the pain as I introduce you to the essentials of accounting. If you already have a good grasp of basic accounting theory, you can skip these chapters and move on to Chapter 5.

Basic Accounting: The Grammar of Cash-Driver Language

 F YOU ARE NOT FAMILIAR WITH THE FUNDAMENTALS OF accounting—the structure of financial statements, the debit and credit rules of the double-entry system, construction of a cash-flow statement and analysis of ratios—this chapter and the next are absolutely essential. And for those whose understanding of these concepts may be a bit shaky, these chapters can get you up to speed.

This overview of basic accounting will make it far easier to grasp all that follows, starting with the ability to see that although many transactions will affect your cash account as either debits or credits, many others leave cash entirely unaffected. The frequency of each type of transaction, the amounts involved and the timing of each will all affect the degree to which the flow of value differs from the flow of cash. Accounting is the grammar system by which we evaluate and record all the events that ultimately find their way to the *balance sheet* and *income statement*. These two primary financial statements will be examined closely to develop the important insights that flow from their ratio analysis and cash-flow analysis. Once these basics of accounting grammar are in place, you will be ready to focus specifically on each of the seven cash drivers (Chapters 5 through 11).

The Accounting Equation

Simply put, the accounting equation means that everything used by the business has to come initially from either its owners or its creditors. The business entity may be a sole proprietorship, a partnership or some form of corporation, but since the corporate form is most common, we will use it for illustration. Everything the corporation owns—its assets—has to be financed by someone, whether by you or some associates as stockholders, by a bank loan or by a supplier.

At this point, perhaps without realizing it, you have already been exposed to the basic structure of the balance sheet, which is made up of the same three structural pieces just described: what the business owns (total assets), the interest of owners in what's owned (net worth, or owner's equity), and the interest of creditors in what's owned (liabilities).

Let's look at the accounting equation in a slightly different way:

Assets = Liabilities + Net Worth (A = L + NW)

Take a look at the simple balance sheet on the opposite page. Everything the business entity itself owns is placed on the left. Everything it owes goes on the right. Also on the right is the owner's equity, or net-worth accounts, representing the difference between what the entity owns and what it owes. Note that the balance sheet actually balances—that is, the asset side is exactly *balanced* by the other side, consisting of the liabilities and net worth. The accounting equation equates. This fundamental relationship of balance must be maintained.

Anything added for use in the business is an additional asset; it has to have its cost covered by either creditors or owners. Owners may cover such costs by direct investments in the company—that is, by buying stock. More commonly, owners cover the costs of buying assets indirectly, through earnings retained in the business. The accounting equation, A=L+NW, always holds, unless there is an accounting error. (Just because the equation holds and the balance sheet balances that doesn't mean there are no errors. It sometimes happens that something gets recorded under the wrong heading *but* on the

| BOX 3-1 | ABC CO. Balance Sheet 12/31/2000 |

CURRENT ASSETS

Cash	$	5,000
Accounts receivable		50,000
Inventory		75,000
TOTAL CURRENT ASSETS	**$**	**130,000**

FIXED ASSETS

Land	25,000
Office equipment	10,000
Delivery equipment	10,000
Machinery and equipment	80,000
Building and improvements	100,000
GROSS FIXED ASSETS	**$ 225,000**
Less: Accumulated depreciation	55,000
TOTAL FIXED ASSETS (NET)	**$ 170,000**
TOTAL ASSETS	**$ 300,000**

CURRENT LIABILITIES

Notes payable bank	$	5,000
Accounts payable		50,000
TOTAL CURRENT LIABILITIES	**$**	**55,000**

SENIOR LONG-TERM LIABILITIES

Plant mortgage	50,000
Equipment loans	30,000
TOTAL SENIOR LONG-TERM LIABILITIES	**$ 80,000**
TOTAL LIABILITIES	**$ 135,000**

NET WORTH

Common stock	100,000
Retained earnings	65,000
TOTAL NET WORTH	**$ 165,000**
TOTAL LIABILITIES AND NET WORTH	**$ 300,000**

appropriate side of the balance sheet. In that case the balance sheet still balances and the error has to be found some other way. That, however, gets to a level of detail that we don't need to deal with here.)

Now that you understand the basic accounting equation of the balance sheet, it would be helpful to get a preliminary sense of the kind of insights some basic balance-sheet information might suggest in cash-driver terms. Take a moment to study the structure and the contents of the balance sheet on page 35.

Can you see why this is an enterprise with a possible cash problem? The cash balance of $5,000 will quickly be used to pay the short-term note due to the bank. Accounts receivable from customers are being turned into cash day by day as customers pay their bills. But just as quickly as that cash comes in, it must be turned around and sent back out to pay the accounts payable to suppliers. If those suppliers don't get paid as agreed, they will generally stop shipping product (except maybe C.O.D.), leaving you with an inventory reduction that will almost certainly cause a sales decline because you won't have the right quantities in the right mix to meet all your orders.

The Double-Entry System

Standard accrual-accounting systems operate on the basis of what's known as double-entry bookkeeping. Double entry is very descriptive; it is also very logical. It is descriptive because every transaction is recorded twice. It is logical because the two sides to every transaction are central to keeping the two sides of the balance sheet in balance. The double-entry method is the key to keeping things in such balance. But what about income statements—does double-entry accounting work there as well, or do we have to have a different system?

The Balance Sheet / Income Statement Connection

Fortunately, double-entry works just fine for both kinds of statements. Here is how the two connect and interrelate through the magic of double-entry. Although the balance sheet and the income statement are separate and distinct entities, they are closely linked. The linkage from the balance-sheet side is through its net-worth section—on the entry called *retained earnings,* or profit retained in the business. A useful analogy of the balance-sheet/income-statement relationship would be the two sides of the brain, whereby each side has its own areas of specialized function. The two sides, however, work according to the same basic rules and are able to cooperate in many tasks because they are linked via a communication channel called the corpus callosum. Think of that retained-earnings part of the balance sheet as the connection point for one side of the financial corpus callosum. On the income-statement side, the connection to the balance sheet is via the line called net income. It is the point from which income-statement profit gets passed to the ownership account on the balance sheet as part of the end-of-period closing process. The simplified income statement on page 38 illustrates to point.

The Common Rules for Balance-Sheet & Income-Statement Entries

As with computers and digital electronics, accounting's basic rules are binary. Everything in computers and digital electronics is fundamentally based on a switch being on or off, or a charge being positive or negative. Likewise, there are only two options in accounting: We can either debit an account or credit it. Because accounting is a *double-entry* system, we must have equal and opposite charges for the two sides of the balance sheet and each of the two parts—revenue and expense—of the income statement. That balance persists up to and through the point of passing data between the income statement and the balance sheet at the close of the accounting period. Preserving this balance requires that for every transaction there be an arithmetic balance; that is, debits must always exactly equal credits.

The basic rules for the way debits and credits work are really a lot more straightforward than most nonaccountants think. As with so many other areas of expertise, jargon that was invented to deal with specific issues winds up becoming a bar-

BOX 3-2	ABC Co. Income Statement 12 Months Ended 12/31/00

Sales	$	587,456
Cost of Goods Sold		400,000
Depreciation in COGS		14,000
GROSS PROFIT/REVENUES	$	173,456
General & Administrative Expense	$	48,000
Selling Expense		12,000
Officers Compensation		52,000
Depreciation		2,300
TOTAL OPERATING EXPENSES	$	114,300
TOTAL OPERATING PROFIT (gross profit - expenses)	$	59,156
EARNINGS BEFORE INTEREST, TAXES	$	75,456
& DEBT AMORTIZATION (EBITDA)		
(principal repayment)		
EARNINGS BEFORE INTEREST & TAXES (EBIT)	$	59,156
Interest Expense ST (short term, debt		2,300
due in less than one year)		
Interest Expense LTD. (long term debt over one year)		4,100
INTEREST EXPENSE	$	6,400
PROFIT BEFORE TAXES & EXTRAORDINARY ITEMS	$	52,756
Current Taxes		18,766
NET INCOME	$	33,990

rier to understanding by the nonexpert. Humor, though, is often helpful in puncturing such barriers. An often-repeated accounting story tells of the senior partner of a major international accounting firm who began each workday for his entire career with the same ritual. He walked to the far end of the executive conference room next to his office and moved aside the picture of the founder to reveal a wall safe that he proceeded to open. He removed a piece of paper, looked at it briefly, then returned it to the safe. Upon his retirement, the senior partner passed the combination to the safe to his much younger associate, who had been elevated to managing-partner rank. On her first day in the managing partner's office suite, she could barely contain her excitement as she practically ran to the safe, opened it, retrieved the dog-eared scrap of paper and read, "Debits by the door, credits by the window." Though not really *quite* that simple, the basic rules are simple enough to make mastering the concept worth a few minutes of concentration.

Here is the basic debit/credit rule expressed in the form of two definitions. If you want a real mental comfort with basic accounting and the cash-flow issues on which the cash drivers depend, I suggest you go so far as to memorize them:

Debit: any *increase* in an *asset* or *expense* account, *or* any *decrease* in a *liability, net worth* or *revenue* account.
Credit: the opposite of the above; any *decrease* in an *asset* or *expense* account, or any *increase* in a *liability, net worth* or *revenue* account.

The basic rules for the way debits and credits work are really a lot more straightforward than most nonaccountants think. Essentially, for every transaction there must be an arithmetic balance; that is, debits must always exactly equal credits.

The assumption is that buying an asset ultimately takes cash and reducing a debt or liability likewise ultimately takes cash. The reverse is also true. Any decrease in an asset, or increase in an obligation, presumes cash coming in. Once you become comfortable with these basic mechanics and rules of financial-statement structure, along with the debit and credit rules, you will be able to use the cash drivers more effectively and get a handle on cash-flow issues more clearly. Beyond that, however, you will also be in a position to absorb a broad range of financial information and participate effectively in financial discussions as your career and business continue to develop.

Using the Debit and Credit Rules

The most common transaction in a business involves a sale. Because a sale represents revenue, we go ahead and *debit* sales for the amount of the sale—say, $1,000. In fact, though, we did not collect $1,000. Instead, we got $200 down, which increased our cash account—an asset—and we also created an account receivable, thereby increasing that asset due from the customer by the difference of $800. The basic accounting-system entries to begin reflecting this transaction, then, are as follows:

Debit cash:	$200
Debit accounts receivable:	$800
Credit sales:	$1,000

Note that the entries are balanced, as they must be—the debits equal the credits. Yet something doesn't seem right— what about inventory? We have sold something from inventory but haven't accounted for it, even though we know that it decreased by an amount equal to our product *cost*, say $500. Part of the transactional-analysis task in accounting is to be sure that there is an entry for *every* affected account. Since inventory is an asset, we must *credit* it to record a decrease, so we go ahead and credit inventory for $500.

Credit inventory:	$500

But now the debits no longer equal the credits, and that's not OK—the system won't be in balance until we offset the credit entry that reduced inventory by $500 with one (or more) appropriate *debit(s) totaling $500.*

What debit could logically offset the inventory credit of $500?

We know that inventory is an asset, but the actual *use* of inventory is an *expense*—and we did use some. The offset we are looking for, then, must be an expense item. In the earlier discussion of cash-versus accrual-accounting systems, I pointed out that in the cash-based system, you don't really need to record inventory as an asset; you could just expense it as it's purchased. But neither the accounting profession nor the IRS will let you do that, and so accrual accounting becomes the standard. We establish inventory as an asset when we acquire it, regardless of when or how we pay for it. We then expense it only *as used* to fill customer orders. The result in this accrual-based system is that it is the *use* of inventory that is an expense, whereas its original acquisition is an asset creation. The transaction entry, then, is:

Debit cost of goods sold: $500 (an expense), reflecting an increase.
Credit inventory: $500 (an asset), reflecting a decrease.

We do, of course, have lots of other costs in the business beyond inventory, so let's further assume that the other expense debits for the period total $450. That covers all of our payroll, occupancy, delivery costs, and so forth. Some of these we have perhaps paid in cash: debit X, Y or Z expense, and credit cash for the same amounts.

Debit X expense:	$150
Debit Y expense:	$150
Debit Z expense:	$150
Credit cash:	$450

In other cases, though, despite having *incurred* the expenses, we have not yet paid for them; in that case we would *accrue* the expense items—for example, debit A, B, or C expense, which affects the income statement, and credit accrued expense—a liability on the balance sheet. Accrued expense is something we actually owe, a liability. Perhaps it is an accrued payroll expense because the payroll checks won't actually be drawn until next month. Perhaps it is an accrued payroll tax we owe to some government entity. An accrued expense, or an accrued liability generally, differs from an account payable in that the payable results from a specific deliverable that someone has supplied, such as inventory, services or supplies. An accrued expense liability more typically results from a service flow provided over a period of time, such as utilities or labor.

If you have been keeping track of profit and loss in the example we have been following in the last few paragraphs, you will have noted a total of $1,000 in revenue and only $950 in expenses against it. In the end-of-period accounting close process, the resultant $50 profit ($1,000 – $950) will be transferred from the income statement to the retained-earnings account within the net-worth section of the balance sheet. Then the accounting cycle can begin anew for the next period, with a brand new income statement and a continued further updating of the balance sheet.

The Nature of the Balance Sheet & Income Statement

Each income statement and balance sheet is limited by its very nature to the time period it covers. The income statement shows what happened *during* the time period and might be compared to a video as contrasted with the balance sheet, which is more like a still photo. The profit or loss that the income statement records over the time period is transferred to the balance sheet as of a specific point at the end of the period. This timing distinction suggests that the difference between any two successive balance sheets can be explained by the income statement for the time period *between* those balance-sheet dates. This is illustrated most clearly by reconciling the change in retained earnings between balance-sheet dates to the income statement's reported earnings for the intervening period. As mentioned earlier, the point of connection is the retained-earnings account on the balance-sheet side and net income on the income statement side. The typical form this connection takes is quite simple:

> **Retained earnings** (on balance sheet of 12/31/00)
> + **Net income** (calendar 2001 income statement)
> − **Common- and preferred-stock dividends** (from 2001 income statement)
>
> = **Retained earnings** (on balance sheet of 12/31/01)

The balance sheet and income statement are necessarily summary in nature and are put together to help evaluate what went on during the accounting period. They are not themselves everyday working documents but are constructed periodically from the daily records of the business. That daily record-keeping process typically begins with the original records of each sale, invoice, receipt and disbursement. There are also so-called adjusting entries to reflect changes in accounts, such as increases and decreases in longer-term assets that have no near-term cash effects. The information from these original-transaction documents is then entered in a journal from which it is later transferred, or posted, to ledgers containing records of the individual balance-sheet and income-statement line items. If all the ledger balances add up so that total debit balance items equal total credit balance items at the end of the period, then the trial balance process is complete. Then, and only then, may the total from each ledger be moved into its appropriate spot on the balance sheet and income statement.

An interesting and instructive feature to think about when looking at the structure of balance sheets and income statements is their relative shapes. For example, a balance sheet can be somewhat top-heavy, as in the case of a high-value, low-inventory-turnover business such as a jewelry store. At the other extreme might be a real-estate-based business such as ownership of a nursing home, in which fixed assets are the overwhelmingly dominant part of the balance sheet. The jewelry store could easily have 85% or more of its assets in inventory, which would appear as a current asset near the top of the balance sheet. The nursing-home owner, by contrast, might have 85% or more of its assets in the long-term category of real estate, near the bottom of the balance sheet. It's sort of like the shape of Eddie Murphy in *The Nutty Professor* as contrasted, perhaps, with Dolly Parton's jewelry store.

A great many nursing homes, however, are not operated by their owners, but are leased to professional operators. Such an operator would typically own no real estate but might have considerable inventory in both short-term asset categories (such as consumables like food, sheets and supplies) and in long-term assets (such as furniture, medical equipment, vehicles and leasehold improvements). We might think of such a muscular balance sheet as a veritable Arnold Schwarzenegger in contrast with the anemic Woody Allens found among many high-tech software and dot-com companies.

The shape of the asset side of the balance sheet will ordinarily indicate a lot about the liability side as well. The reason is that there is basic good sense in matching financing duration to the useful life of the asset type being financed. Generally, this means financing short-term assets with short-term liabilities and longer-term assets with longer-term liabilities. Your accounts-payable values will spontaneously and organically follow and track with inventory in most businesses. Real estate assets and their long-term mortgage financing will naturally tend to track with one another. Perhaps your business is seasonal in nature. You may have wide swings in inventory and accounts receivable over the course of the year, so your banker will not want to finance those with a five-year term loan. What you need instead is a revolving line of credit that peaks at the top of your season and is fully repaid by the time your slow season returns.

The shape of the asset side of the balance sheet will ordinarily indicate a lot about the liability side as well.

Just as there are different shapes to balance sheets, there are different shapes to income statements. The jewelry store, for example, will typically have very high gross margins to compensate for its big investment in inventory. The higher gross margins help compensate for a long inventory-holding period, together with some level of fashion-related risks and little financial leverage. An automobile dealer, on the other hand, will have extremely thin gross margins because there is relatively low value added, a fairly short inventory-holding period, high leverage and not much risk of deep inventory losses.

Supermarkets are another interesting case in this regard. They have gross margins far lower than jewelers and lower still than most other retailers except automobile dealers. When all of the supermarket's costs have been covered, net margins turn out to be extraordinarily low. That is the thin side, the income-statement side, of this business. The saving grace comes on the balance-sheet side, where supermarket inventory investment turns out to be equally thin. The key feature of supermarket inventory is that it turns over rapidly—so much so that, although the net margins are often down in the 1% range, the supermarket gets its margins many times over in the course of the year: perhaps 90 times on its investment in milk inventory, 75 times on meat, 40 times on cereals and 30 times on paper goods. Because of this inverse relationship between turnover and margins, we would expect milk to carry a lower margin than meat, meat lower than cereals and cereals lower than paper goods. This, of course, turns out to be the case because from a financial point of view, the return on any product is an economic function of the cash dollars invested and expensed, not anything intrinsic to the product or service per se, despite the fact that milk and cereal are natural allies.

One of the most useful tools for evaluating the shape of balance sheets and income statements is to consider them on a common-sized basis; one that is expressed in percentages rather than dollars.

COMMON SIZING

One of the most useful tools for evaluating the shape of balance sheets and income statements is to consider them on a *common-sized* basis; one that is expressed in percentages rather than dollars. The income statement thus begins with sales or revenue as 100%, and every other line item then becomes a percentage of sales or revenue. Similarly, the common-sized balance sheet is geared to total assets so that each line item is presented as a percentage of total assets.

There are two ways in particular that this common-sized approach can help you manage cash flow. First, the common-sized statements bring out period-to-period changes, showing which categories of assets and expenses seem to be growing faster than others. Second, the common-sized statements help put the five main cash sources that correspond to the financial-statement blocks into perspective, showing their relative importance. The structure of the financial statement yields only five basic elements: assets, liabilities and net worth from the balance sheet; and revenue and expense from the income statement. By examining these categories and their subparts on the comparative basis permitted by common sizing, you can often discern broad options more clearly and identify opportunities for improvement more easily. This works with individual line items as well as the five large blocks. If, for example, you see that a certain category of asset has risen from 5% to 7% of total assets, you can more readily flag it as a potential area to liberate cash—that is, improve cash flow.

Any period-to-period increase in an asset account or decrease in a liability or net-worth item is to be considered cash flowing out. The assumption is that buying an asset ultimately takes cash and reducing a debt or liability likewise ultimately takes cash.

As this discussion of the balance sheet and income statement moves toward a more explicitly cash-flow orientation, remember that any period-to-period increase in an asset account or decrease in a liability or net-worth item is to be considered cash flowing out. You are looking for possible fuel sources, places you can use as cash filling stations. On the income statement, the options are easier to see—that is, decreased expenses or improved margins.

Here is a summary of the five basic financial-statement blocks and associated cash-generating options, along with a couple of examples of each:

FROM THE BALANCE SHEET

- **Sell or convert assets to cash:** Sell a surplus delivery truck for cash, or collect faster than usual on an account receivable.
- **Borrow or increase liabilities:** Borrow cash from the bank, or receive inventory from a major supplier on longer-than-traditional terms.
- **Sell equity:** Sell stock or a partnership interest for cash.

FROM THE INCOME STATEMENT

- **Increase product profit margins:** Negotiate a better quantity discount from a supplier to bring costs down, or raise prices without losing sales by persuading customers that the quality you're delivering is worth the higher price.
- **Decrease operating-expense ratios:** Reduce selling expense by use of telemarketing to attract a large number of small customers, or increase sales volume without a related rise in certain fixed costs such as senior-management salaries.

Each of these options can be thought of as cash being pumped into the enterprise, or if the flow goes the opposite direction from the examples described, they become additional fuel burned up in the journey through the accounting period. These five are the *only* options for fuel generation. Within each structural category there may be many choices, many different ways to pump that particular grade of cash, but there are only the five basic grades. Depending on your role in the business, you may have many or few options as to what you can do to affect cash flow, but practically everyone has some opportunity to contribute.

Statements of Cash Flow & Analysis of Ratios

S WE HAVE ALREADY DISCUSSED, THE INCOME statement by itself only hints at the cash-flow story. It offers no insight into where cash came from or how it was used, recording only two structural elements, revenue and expense, which track flows of value, not cash. The cash-flow statement integrates the income-statement data with the additional information provided by the balance sheets to get the full story. Note that *balance sheets* here is intentionally plural—double the fun. The cash-flow statement tracks the underlying cash events behind the balance sheets and income statement, whose accrual numbers present only an *as though* cash truth. The statement of cash flow offers actual cash truth.

To prepare a cash-flow statement, you need three things: a starting balance sheet, an ending balance sheet and an income statement for the time in between. With these statements, you can adjust each major-value line item from the income statement by the *change* in its most closely associated balance-sheet items to determine what actually happened in cash terms. By such adjustments, you undo the misleading *as though cash* assumption built into accrual-based accounting systems. For example, let's look at Jones Dynamite Co. for the second quarter of 2000, ending 6/30/00.

> **2nd quarter sales** (per income statement) $2,125,500
> **+ Beginning accounts receivable** (per 3/31 balance sheet)
> $1,275,500
>   (assumed paid in 2nd quarter)
> **– Ending accounts receivable** (per 6/30 balance sheet)
> $1,365,500
>   (not yet collected)
> **= Cash from sales in 2nd quarter** $2,035,500

To complete the cash-flow statement, you would proceed line by line, capturing all the changes in the income statement's and balance-sheets' elements, showing where cash came from and how it was used during the accounting period. The process follows the income-statement sequence as though everything had been settled in cash *but then immediately reverses* the misleading *as though* assumption. This reversal requires that every income-statement line item be adjusted for the period-to-period change in the related balance-sheet line items. Let's examine that adjusting logic more closely.

The Cash-Adjusted Income Statement

The process of creating the cash-flow statement starts at the top of the income statement with the accrual-based sales number as the first step toward getting the actual *cash from sales* figure, as in the example above. This cash-adjusted income statement is the most logical form for a cash-flow statement. It's *cash-adjusted* in the sense that we always presume that an increase in an asset or a decrease in a liability or net-worth account represents cash flowing out, and vice versa. Let's examine that plus-and-minus logic a bit more closely. As we do, look at the Uniform Credit Analysis® (UCA) cash-flow worksheet on pages 52 and 53. This format is recommended by the Risk Management Association, the primary trade group for commercial bankers. Bankers succeed in business largely by getting back the money they lent, so their interest in cash flow is intense. To help ensure success, they have standardized this interrelating of balance sheet and associated income-statement line items to create what I think is the most useful of the available cash-flow-statement formats.

In a pure cash system, the only way to get anything that might be considered an asset is to buy it for cash, and the only way to reduce a debt is to pay it off in cash. The only way to decrease net worth is to pay it out as a dividend or lose it through a negative net-profit figure. The consequence of such direct-cash happenings is that all increases in assets and all decreases in either liabilities or net worth between balance-sheet dates necessarily imply cash outflows. For that reason the cash-flow statement adjusts the related income-statement line from *both* ends of the time horizon—that is, the starting and ending balance sheets. Note, too, that opposite movements in these balance-sheet items imply cash flowing *in* so that, for example, a decrease in the asset *inventory* from one balance sheet to the next implies that cash came in in an amount equal to the excess of inventory use (to meet customer orders) over inventory acquisition.

While the balance sheet and income statement are constructed—that is, built up from the transaction level as sales and other business events are recorded in a journal and then successively carried over to ledgers, trial balance sheets and finished statements—the cash-flow statement is deconstructed.

While the balance sheet and income statement are constructed—that is, built up from the transaction level as sales and other business events are recorded in a journal and then successively carried over to ledgers, trial balance sheets and finished statements—the cash-flow statement is deconstructed. Instead of assembling a cash flow from the ground up, the balance sheet and income statement are deconstructed into their components, then rearranged to tell the story of cash flow from pieces that were originally put together to tell the story of value flow. Knowing and understanding the value-flow story is important, of course, but it is incomplete without an understanding of the cash-flow story.

Because of my emphasis on cash flow, you may get the impression that standard, accrual-based balance sheets and income statements are of little value, but that is not the case.

(continued on page 54)

BOX 4-1 | **Uniform Credit Analysis® Cash-Flow Worksheet**

ACCOUNT TITLE	LOCATION	CASH IMPACT	
Sales	Income statement	(+)	$ _____
Accounts receivable	Balance sheet	decrease (+), increase (-)	_____
Cash from sales			_____
Cost of goods sold (COGS)	Income statement	(-)	
Depreciation in COGS*	Income statement	(+)	
Inventory	Balance sheet	decrease (+), increase (-)	_____
Accounts payable	Balance sheet	increase (+), decrease (-)	_____
Cash production costs			_____

Cash from sales – Cash production costs = **Gross cash profit** _____

Selling, General & Administrative Expense (SG&A)	Income statement	(-)	_____
Depreciation & amortization in SG&A*	Income statement	(+)	_____
Prepaids & deposits	Balance sheet	decrease (+), increase (-)	_____
Accrued liabilities	Balance sheet	increase (+), decrease (-)	_____
Cash Operating Expenses			_____

Gross cash profit – Cash operating expenses = **Cash after operations** _____

Other income	Income statement	(+)	_____
Other expenses	Income statement	(-)	_____
Other current assets	Balance sheet	decrease (+), increase (-)	_____
Other current liabilities	Balance sheet	increase (+), decrease (-)	_____
Other assets	Balance sheet	decrease (+), increase (-)	_____
Other liabilities	Balance sheet	increase (+), decrease (-)	_____
Miscellaneous cash income/expenses			
Tax provision (benefit)	Income statement	benefit (+), provision (-)	_____
Income tax refund receivable	Balance sheet	decrease (+), increase (-)	_____
Deferred tax benefit (asset)	Balance sheet	decrease (+), increase (-)	_____
Income taxes payable	Balance sheet	increase (+), decrease (-)	_____
Deferred taxes payable	Balance sheet	increase (+), decrease (-)	_____
Cash taxes paid			_____

Cash after operations + Miscellaneous cash income ÷ expenses +

Cash taxes paid = **Net cash after operations** _____

Interest expense	Income statement	(-)	_____
Dividends or owners' withdrawal	Income statement	(-)	_____

Dividends payable	Balance sheet	increase (+), decrease (-)	_____
Financing costs			_____
Net cash after operations – Financing costs = **Net cash income**			_____
Current maturities long-term debt (prior year)	Balance sheet	(-)	_____
Current capital lease obligation (prior year)	Balance sheet	(-)	_____
Scheduled debt amortization			_____
Net cash income – Scheduled debt amortization = **Cash after debt amortization**			_____
Fixed assets, net	Balance sheet	decrease (+), increase (-)	
Intangibles	Balance sheet	decrease (+), increase (-)	
Depreciation and amortization*	Income statement	(-)	
Capital spending, net			_____
Investment	Balance sheet	decrease (+), increase (-)	
Total capital spending and investment, net			
Cash after debt amortization – Total capital spending and investment, net = **Financing requirement**			_____
Short-term debt	Balance sheet	increase (+), decrease (-)	_____
Long-term debt	Balance sheet	increase (+), decrease (-)	_____
(excluding prior year's current maturities)			
Preferred stock	Balance sheet	increase (+), decrease (-)	_____
Common stock	Balance sheet	increase (+), decrease (-)	_____
Paid in capital	Balance sheet	increase (+), decrease (-)	_____
Treasury stock	Balance sheet	decrease (+), increase (-)	_____
Total Financing			
Financing requirement – Total financing = Calculated change in cash			_____
Cash & equivalent	Balance sheet	increase (+), decrease (-)	_____
Marketable securities	Balance sheet	increase (+), decrease (-)	_____
Actual change in cash			_____
Calculated change in cash = **Actual change in cash**			_____

* Note: Where necessary details regarding depreciation and amortization are not provided on the face of the income statement, you may have to refer to footnotes and/or the statement of changes if provided.

We need both melody and harmony. There are actually some real limitations to looking only at cash-flow issues and cash-flow statements. If cash flow were the only issue of significance, no one would bother with the

Because of my emphasis on cash flow, you may get the impression that standard, accrual-based balance sheets and income statements are of little value, but that is not the case. We need both melody and harmony.

other statements. You could manage solely by the company's checkbook, in which cash is what it is at any given moment. This, of course, assumes that all receipts and disbursements are entered there on an accurate and timely basis just as with your personal checking account. Of course, few businesses run on such a cash in/cash out basis. Having the additional insights that come in the form of balance-sheet and income-statement data, though,

readily offsets most of the cash-flow-only limitations.

The two most significant things that balance-sheet and income-statement data add to cash-flow information have to do with time horizons. First, balance-sheet dollar figures for items such as inventory and accounts receivable give important insights into likely near-term cash flows. As the business continues its normal cycle of converting inventory to sales to receivables and back to cash again, the inventory and receivables values set expectations for the cash flows from those primary sources. Suppose, for example, that your wholesale auto-parts business has:

$100,000 in inventory;
$200,000 in accounts receivable with gross margins of 50%;
SG&A at 40%;
90 days' worth of inventory; and
45 days of receivables and payables

You can quickly estimate next quarter's approximate level of cash flow from these elements. Here's how: One business quarter is 90 days, so receivables at 45 days turn twice in that period, yielding cash in from receivables of 2 x $200,000 = $400,000. But receivables from new sales at the same selling rate immediately reverse that cash in for a net of zero—although you collect $400,000 from customers in that 90-day period, you also extend another 90 days worth of credit in the same period. However, you do hold on to half of the $400,000, in the form of 50% gross margins totaling $200,000. From that $200,000 in cash gross margin, you pay out 40% of the $400,000 in sales for SG&A expenses totaling $160,000. That leaves you with a net of $40,000 to cover interest expense, taxes, dividends and capital expenditures. And, this assumes no growth in sales, in which case additional cash would be needed to support net growth in receivables and inventory.

The date of the actual payment for transactions is not particularly important for balance sheet and income statement design. Cash-flow statements are where we deal with the payment realities.

The second perspective on timing that traditional balance-sheet and income-statement data add to what cash-flow analysis provides is rooted in the accounting principle known as *matching*. According to this principle, costs associated with producing revenue are matched to the time period in which the revenue-generating activity takes place. The date of the actual payment for these transactions is not particularly important for balance-sheet and income-statement design. Cash-flow statements are where we deal with the payment realities.

Other Cash-Flow Formats

In addition to the cash-adjusted income statement represented by the UCA (Uniform Credit Analysis®) cash-flow-statement format, there are two other generally accepted patterns. Both have been defined by the American Institute of CPAs (AICPA) and balance, as does the UCA format, to the actual change in cash during the period. The AICPA's Financial Accounting Standards Board's (FASB) two alternative cash-flow statement formats are presented in the boxes on pages 56 and 57 as the playfully descriptive Direct and Indirect methods.

Each format begins with cash flow from operating activities, moves through to cash from investing activities and final-

---

BOX 4-2	Cash Flow: Direct Method	

Cash flows from operating activities
Cash from sales	$33,506,676
Cash production costs	(28,794,388)
Cash operating expenses	(3,186,992)
Interest expense, net	(544,082)
Taxes paid	(31,346)
Misc. cash income/expense	82,024
Net cash provided by operating activities	**$41,094,584**
Cash flows from investing activities	
Capital spending/long-term investments	$ (676,739
Net cash used in investing activities	**$ (676,739)**
Cash flows from financing activities	
Change in short-term financing	$(572,376)
Change in long-term financing	(29,082)
Change in equity	171,069
Net cash from financing	**$(430,389)**
Net increase in cash	**$(12,544)**
Actual change in cash	**$(12,544)**

ly to cash from financing activities. The *direct* method begins at cash from operating activities starting with cash from sales, whereas the *indirect* method begins with net income. The direct method has the advantage of being a better parallel with the actual operational flow of the business. The indirect method is preferred by some because of its more traditional approach that is rooted in a well-established accounting rule of thumb for cash-flow estimation, whereby net income and depreciation (as well as any other expenses that have no direct cash implications) are added together. In both the direct and indirect methods, there is a line called *cash from operating activities*, which is generally identical to what is called *net cash income* on the UCA cash-flow format. When this operating cash-flow number is reduced by capital expenditures, the result is referred to as *free cash flow*. That term is worth noting for its content value as well as because it is one of the few reasonably

BOX 4-3 **Cash Flow: Indirect Method**	
Net income	**$223,308**
Adjustments to reconcile:	
Depreciation, amortization	$338,233
Fixed asset adjustment	(12,411)
Undistributed earnings	(52,136)
Change in accounts receivable	(197,442)
Change in inventory	(46,298)
Change in prepaids	37,905
Change in other current assets	12,243
Change in account payable	372,267
Change in accrued liabilities	226,471
Change in other current liabilities	140,000
Change in non-current income	52,444
Net cash provided by operating activities	**$1,094,584**
Cash flows from investing activities	
Capital spending/long-term investments	$(676,739)
Net cash used in investing activities	**$(676,739)**
Cash flows from financing activities	
Change in short-term financing	$(572,376)
Change in long-term financing	(29,082)
Change in equity	171,069
Net cash from financing activities	**$ 430,389**
Net increase in cash	**$(12,544)**
Actual change in cash	**$(12,544)**

well accepted terms in the field of cash-flow analysis; it is essentially identical to cash after debt amortization from the UCA cash-flow format.

The basic idea behind the starting point of the indirect method is that net income in a stable world ought to be available in cash. The main exception would be an adjustment for those expenses incurred for accounting purposes though not involving an actual *expenditure* during the period. Examples include depreciation, depletion, amortization and a variety of expenses *reserved for*, such as future warranty costs. Since these not-yet-spent costs have already been subtracted in calculating net income, the idea is that they need to be *added back* to get cash flow.

But under what circumstances does the traditional "cash flow equals net income plus depreciation" rule of thumb actually work? The answer is that it is absolutely accurate under only one set of circumstances. It works only under conditions of absolute structural stability, when every balance sheet and income-statement line item remains perfectly proportionally the same. (or if whatever changes do take place should happen to offset one another exactly). This implies a world of either great stability or incredible coincidence. Neither is a typical business experience.

> **The traditional "cash flow equals net income plus depreciation" rule of thumb actually works under only one set of circumstances— conditions of absolute structural stability, when every balance sheet and income-statement line item remains perfectly proportionally the same.**

In the 1950s, when many of today's retiring senior executives were being educated, the American business scene was much more stable. Over the years, however, the pace of business has accelerated and become subject to many more changes, both internal and external. Options have multiplied, the range of competitors has expanded, the rate of new-product introduction has exploded, and the role of foreign firms in the array of suppliers, customers and competitors has gone beyond anything the manager of the '50s might have imagined. We have seen and will continue to see new kinds of business combinations and techniques as adaptation to changing technology and conditions continues. Integration vertically, horizontally and otherwise will ebb and flow. Conglomeration in various forms and guises will recur. New cross-border and cross-technology combinations will develop. Distribution-channel patterns and industry definitions are shifting in response to deregulation, technology and consolidation. Rules of thumb based on assumptions of stability, therefore, have become downright dangerous in most cases. With this as background, let's now examine the case for the use of the UCA Cash-Flow Statement over the FASB direct or indirect methods that we have also considered.

Why the UCA Cash-Flow Format Is Preferred

The UCA format was developed in the 1970s by Wells Fargo Bank and promulgated through the banking industry by Robert Morris Associates (now the Risk Management Association), which operates to exchange both information and insights regarding commercial-lending activity. The problem that bankers were addressing was basically one of movement from stability to nonstability. Better tools were needed to analyze the creditworthiness of borrowers in a more complex world in which the old rules of thumb were no longer reliable.

One of the signal examples of the need for new accounting tools was the W.T. Grant debacle. Long an American retail institution, this huge company had undergone a series of changes in performance, strategy and environmental pressures that created an enormous gap between traditional rule-of-thumb cash flow and true cash flow. The big, prestigious money-center corporate lenders who had a piece of the W.T. Grant debt package were focused on the rule-of-thumb cash-flow number and were badly thrown when the company declared bankruptcy. (Like many things in life, though, bankruptcy can be more or less severe depending on circumstances. Later in this chapter, we will take a look at the two basic types of bankruptcy both as a warning and as another perspective on the centrality of cash-flow management.)

The UCA cash-flow format was designed primarily with the lender in mind. A major advantage for the lender is that it focuses on net-cash income to determine whether the company is liquid on an operating basis. A current ratio or a quick ratio tries to answer that question from a static balance-sheet point of view by relating current assets to current liabilities. But bankers also need to know the answer from an operating perspective. That is to say, did the enterprise cover all cash operating costs and outflows and pay interest on its debt from internally generated fuel? If the net-cash income line on the UCA cash-flow statement is positive, the answer is yes. The same is true of the net cash from operations lines on the other two cash-flow statement formats.

A lender is even more interested in there being a clear enough and large enough expectation of a "yes" at the net-cash income line over the coming periods to ensure debt repayment as scheduled. If net-cash income isn't positive in the historical analysis, there may be little reason to think it will be in the future. Most first-rate lenders today expect to see reasonable business projections that show positive net-cash income adequate to service proposed debt. Another key focus of the UCA format, but one not satisfactorily covered in either of the other formats, is the line called *cash after debt amortization*. This shows whether the company was able to repay debt as scheduled from internally generated sources.

The UCA format is helpful to virtually anyone looking at the firm, not just lenders. That's because it is a cash-adjusted income statement, making it both familiar in its flow sequence and logical in its exposition of how the company normally operates.

The UCA format is helpful to virtually anyone looking at the firm, not just lenders. That's because it *is* a cash-adjusted income statement, making it both familiar in its flow sequence and logical in its exposition of how the company normally operates. When you are approaching lenders, it is always helpful to have information in the form that most directly addresses their concerns. And positive cash projections at the cash-after-debt-amortization line on the UCA cash-flow statement give a positive answer to their critical concern about whether the company prospectively can generate enough cash to pay actual or projected debt as scheduled. This assumes, of course, that the cash-driver assumptions behind the projections are believable.

Long-Term Viability & Cash Flow

Revenue growth is a positive sign of your organization's ability to meet a societal need. Growth, therefore, represents some prima facie evidence that your organization is doing something worthwhile. But there is a check on this process. The check is sustainability, the power to keep on going. Cash flow is the way that this check becomes active. No cash, no go. If your customers, prospects, supporters, patrons, taxpayers or whoever provides your revenue don't provide enough of it, in cash, to cover your costs quickly enough, the organization must radically change. Your company must retrench, merge, sell off assets or otherwise stop being what it was and either curtail its operations or rethink its viability.

There is an old saying that if you don't know where you are going, any road will get you there. A great many businesses operate by that concept. The majority, fortunately, do not. But even in those businesses with a fairly clear plan of where and how they are moving, the cash dimensions of that forward motion are often still pretty fuzzy. It is a rare business in which all the key people know where their firm is headed, why it is taking that particular direction, and what the cash implications of that movement actually look like. If top management is the only place where that information and sensitivity reside, there will be a lack of focus and energy as many key people below that level wander along other roads.

Management owes it to the business owners and to every key management and supervisory employee to define a set of cash-driver objectives.

At the very least, management owes it to the business owners and to every key management and supervisory employee to define a set of cash-driver objectives. These should be well communicated, achievable and logically explained in terms of the individual's job description and sphere of influence. When this occurs, the organization is optimally positioned for growth--not just sales growth, which is not necessarily a good thing, but real growth—an increasing rate of growth in the firm's value. Stated another way, key employees who understand the cash-flow goals and implications of their choices will almost always maximize the company's total economic value. That value is ultimately rooted in the ability to generate increasing cash flows over the long term.

Positive cash flow is the measure of sustainability even in the public sector and in nonprofit organizations. Excess cash may come directly from operations, or be provided by people or organizations who value what an organization does enough to keep it supplied with the fuel to keep things running. In business, those people are the customers. In the public sector they are primarily taxpayers or other political constituencies. In nonprofit organizations, they are usually a combination of users and donors. Regardless of your work setting, cash flow remains the bottom line

Other Measures of a Company's Well Being

With all of this emphasis on cash flow, you may well wonder about other tests, measures and signs of an organization's well-being. Should you disregard more traditional methods of analysis and consider only cash flow? Certainly not. Profitability is still important. How efficiently you utilize your assets needs to be addressed. Questions of leverage regarding how well you use your funds still need to be answered. And clearly, of course, you must be intensely concerned about liquidity in order to quantify the ability to meet short-term financial obligations. These four traditional categories for general financial evaluation—which can be conveniently remembered using the acronym PELL for Profitability, Efficiency, Leverage and Liquidity—all also have cash-flow implications.

Profitability

The simplest way to think about profitability for cash-flow purposes is to focus on three elements: gross margin, operating-expense ratio and rule-of-thumb cash flow. Let's take the last item first. Because of the unusual simplifying assumptions as to stability that rule-of-thumb cash flow requires to be an adequate measure, I recommend its use only in one very restricted circumstance—with those rare companies in which the cash drivers are virtually the same from year to year.

The two other profitability measures are ones already identified as cash drivers: gross margin as a percentage of sales, and operating expense (SG&A) as a percentage of sales. Whatever money remains from each sales dollar after paying cost of goods sold and SG&A is called *cushion*. Cushion is what's left from the business to pay your three most important constituencies: your banker, your government and your stockholders. If margins should erode for reasons beyond your control, cushion can perhaps be shored up by better control of SG&A. Conversely, if SG&A is unavoidably increasing, you can look to gross margin to make up the difference either via pricing or via production and purchasing efficiencies. Maintaining cushion is critical or you'll risk your ability to meet the needs of those three constituencies. Let's look at the long term for Woody's Lumber on a common-sized basis going back to 1989 and tracking though to 2000.

SALES	**100%**
Less: cost of goods sold	(52)%
Leaves: gross margin	48%
Less: operating expense (SG&A)	(30)%
EQUALS: cushion:	**18 %**
Less: interest expense (your banker)	(5)%
taxes (your government)	(4)%
dividends (your stockholders)	(4)%
NET INCOME (after taxes and dividends)	**5%**

Woody's cushion—what was left from each sales dollar after paying cost of goods sold and SG&A—immediately began to shrink, year by year, from the 18% shown above. Over the next five years, from 1990 to 1994, the cushion dropped to 10.5% at an average rate of 1.5 percentage points annually. Interest and dividends stayed about the same, and taxes dropped because of the net-income drop. There are lots of possibilities that might explain what was happening, of course, but the problem in this case was *not* primarily one of operating management.

In Woody's case those responsible for the day-to-day operation of the business were doing excellent work under deteriorating market conditions, in a soft economy and with significant new competition. They tried reducing SG&A and increasing gross margins with little success. The real problem was not operating management but senior management. (In your company, the two management categories may be the same group of people, but that is not the issue. The issue is the quality of the job being done in each category.)

Senior management's job is to stay ahead of the curve, to insure a stream of fresh opportunities to replace those that are growing weary. If the company has traditionally paid out significant dividends, it is a likely sign that senior management has not been particularly concerned with investing in new directions.

Senior management's tasks are both less immediate and less operationally oriented than other business tasks. Its job is to stay ahead of the curve, to ensure a stream of fresh opportunities to replace those that are growing weary. If the company has traditionally paid out significant dividends, it is a likely sign that senior management has not been particularly concerned with investing in new directions. Perhaps the senior management team is hoping to prop up the company's stock price with relatively high dividends in lieu of doing the harder work of finding high-return investment opportunities. Those opportunities must be sought in repositioning the company to meet the challenge of new products, new markets, new processes and new technological applications.

In Woody's case, senior management failed to meet its responsibilities from '89 to '94. As the economy rebounded, things improved somewhat in late '94 and into '95, but the real gain came as new senior management started remaking the company in late '95 and early '96 with a combination of initiatives. These managers relocated most storage to a lower-rent warehouse that was also considerably more labor-efficient. They used the savings from that move to cover increases in delivery costs and tripled their retail space in the original location by remodeling what had previously been expensive storage. They used the additional space for a greatly broadened range of higher-margin home-improvement products. Computer-imaging design-center tools helped both sell and document a greatly increased average sale size through a home-design consulting emphasis that transformed much of the company's basic sales process. By 2000, Woody's had rebounded 20% beyond its late-'80s cushion level. It could have done so considerably earlier, however, had senior management understood the erosion of cushion as a sign that the basics of the business were changing and that strategic rather than merely tactical responses were required.

When it comes to evaluating longer-term profit potential, two ratios to be watched are the dividend-payout ratio and the capital-expenditure ratio. The dividend-payout ratio should be declining as the company invests for innovative growth. The capital-expenditure ratio should be rising, most especially for items related to development of new opportunities.

When it comes to evaluating longer-term profit potential, two ratios to be watched are the dividend-payout ratio and the capital-expenditure ratio. The dividend-payout ratio should be declining as the company invests for innovative growth. The capital-expenditure ratio should be rising.

Efficiency

Asset utilization has many aspects, and there are several measures that may logically be used to gauge efficiency. Most important from an operating-cash-flow point of view are those asset-efficiency measures relating to inventory and accounts receivable. As explained earlier, these are most commonly measured in days. How many days worth of sales are in accounts receivable, and how many days worth of cost of goods sold are in inventory?

These are both relative, or proportional, measures. Generally, as sales go up, the investment in inventory and accounts receivable tends to go up proportionally, thereby keeping the days measure the same. For example: If the average balance of outstanding accounts receivable is one-eighth of annual sales, then days receivable are $\frac{1}{8}$ x 365 days = 46 days. Similarly for inventory: If average inventory value on hand is one-sixth of annual cost of goods sold, then days inventory are $\frac{1}{6}$ x 365 days = 61 days.

This measure in days is a relative measure, which makes it ideal for period-to-period comparisons. It is far more useful than simply comparing absolute dollar values, which could easily be affected by other variables, including such things as growth, seasonality or other issues having no basic connection to the policies and practices by which receivables or inventory are managed. Other things being equal, the goal is to manage asset days (inventory or receivables) downward and liability days (payables) upward for maximizing cash flow. Although there is no necessary connection between these days measures, the underlying issues can certainly be intertwined. If, for example, one of your major suppliers offers longer-than-usual terms for especially large purchases, then your inventory days and payables days are likely to both move upward proportionally. If, on the other hand, the offer isn't longer terms but significantly lower prices on large buys, your inventory days will go up, payables will move little and the impact will register mostly in improved gross margins, unless, of course, you pass along the savings. And if you do pass along the savings, you may well wind up with a spike in sales. Everything that happens with a cash driver has to affect some other measure someplace.

The most important measures of asset efficiency from an operating cash-flow point of view are those relating to inventory and accounts receivable.

There is an offset to these asset-efficiency measures on the liability side of the balance sheet in the form of accounts payable. Since accounts payable consist primarily of amounts owed to suppliers, they can be considered as offsets to the investment in inventory. Because of this, days payable should be included in your evaluation of asset efficiency. Payables, though a liability, are a sort of contra-inventory account. Although logically grouped here as asset-efficiency measures, these three ratios are somewhat better known as *activity ratios* because they do, indeed, say much about turnover or activity rates.

Cash itself is another item of asset efficiency. Unless there is some particular reason for building cash balances, such as anticipated acquisitions, cash balances should be no higher than required to be sure that bills can be paid as they come due. Cash balances earning bank interest pay little in income. Investing that cash in the main operating and developmental areas of the business should always produce far higher returns.

Return on assets is another broad asset-efficiency measure. Its calculation is simply net income divided by assets, and it indicates how efficiently the assets have been deployed for the production of income. So, for example, if net income after tax is $500,000 and total assets are $5,000,000, then return on assets is 10%. If we turn this measure upside down, it tells us how many dollars of assets it takes to generate a dollar of profit. In this example, it would be $10. Either way, efficiency of asset use for producing income is the measure in view.

Cash itself is another item of asset efficiency. Unless there is some particular reason for building cash balances, such as anticipated acquisitions, cash balances should be no higher than required to be sure that bills can be paid as they come due.

The final measure of asset efficiency is assets divided by sales. Here the focus is the investment in assets required to generate a dollar of sales. Because each sale represents a profit opportunity, this ratio reveals something about asset efficiency from a marketing perspective. The goal, obviously, is to get more sales from each dollar of assets employed, thus increasing the return on investment.

In addition to using and managing assets more efficiently, there is a specific financing dimension to asset efficiency: It is not always necessary to own an asset to use it, and it is possible to lease an asset without having it appear on the balance sheet. While leases that are effectively financing exercises have to be capitalized—that is, put on the books as both an asset in use and a liability to be paid—operating leases and rental arrangements permit use of assets without balance-sheet impacts. This can have a positive effect on return on assets by reducing the asset base below what it would be if the asset were owned outright or capitalized on the books as a financing lease. The trade-off is that you may actually pay more for the use of something owned by someone else than you would if you owned it yourself. The lease-versus-buy decision needs to be carefully analyzed.

There is still another, high-level dimension to the asset-owning issue when it comes to efficiency of asset use. Rather than either owning or renting, you may be better off contracting out the entire function. Take the following example. A fresh-fish wholesaler on the Great Lakes is located in the far north and has always relied on its fleet of three trucks to deliver to major metropolitan areas. But all three trucks are now reaching an age and mileage level at which it is time to replace them. A local dealership has offered an operating-lease arrangement that will keep the new trucks off the wholesaler's books and require no up-front cash outlay. The owners are naturally very interested. The extra cash freed up by such a lease will help them with the working capital they need to start a new export line of whitefish caviar.

> **In most small companies, especially closely-held family businesses, the scarcest resource of all, even scarcer than capital, is *management time*.**

In most small companies, especially closely held family businesses such as this one, the scarcest resource of all, even scarcer than capital, is *management time*. The fish wholesaler's managers know the fish business. They spend a lot of time cultivating and maintaining relationships with their somewhat independent Native American sources of supply and their big-city restaurant and broker buyers. They carefully monitor product quality and handling. New developments in packaging and product-line extensions to include other fish and fish-related products are becoming more important. These are the most essential operating and developmental elements of their business. If the company is to grow, more management attention must be focused on these items.

After careful analysis—isolating the transportation issues realistically and substantially from these other higher-level management tasks—the company concluded that contracting out the shipping entirely, rather than leasing or buying new trucks, would be a good choice. Over an 18-month period, the company phased itself out of the shipping business. In doing so, it freed up nearly 20% of the two owners' time to focus on the company's true area of primary value creation, which has almost nothing to do with overseeing the scheduling, maintaining, supervising and driving of trucks. Here the asset-efficiency issue went far beyond how well trucks were used or how well the truck-financing decisions were made. Ultimately, the most important assets of this and other businesses are the skills and knowledge of the people who best understand the dynamics of the business and the directions for its future success. A clear focus on critical core competencies may well be the most asset-efficient direction any company can develop.

Leverage

The primary issue with leverage has to do not with how efficiently you use assets but with how efficiently you use your net worth, or equity, to multiply—or leverage—your investment. In other words, the profit your business returns on equity or net worth should be higher than its return on assets in proportion to your use of borrowed money to fund your business.

Too much leverage, though, puts both your organization and its creditors at risk. Too many liabilities can put your back to the wall quickly if a few things start to go against you. Bankers may call in their loans, suppliers won't ship product, and good employees may look elsewhere. The employee risk is even greater if the company is not seen as able to meet its payroll consistently, or if it is not perceived as staying competitive technologically. Your highly mobile knowledge workers want to be at least on the cutting edge, if not the bleeding edge, of their fields. If your firm can't offer that opportunity technologically, you may well lose the best, the brightest and the highest-initiative people on your staff. Too much leverage exposes you to the risk of not having enough of a financial shock-absorber to get over the potholes that every business encounters. In the other direction, too little leverage can force return on equity below industry norms to the point of making you less competitive.

The cash-flow implications here are simple. The greater the

> **The primary issue with leverage has to do not with how efficiently you use assets, but how efficiently you use your net worth, or equity, to multiply—or leverage—your investment.**

leverage, the greater the risk that other people's fears and decisions can pull the plug. The lower the leverage, the lower the return available to owners of the business. The right leverage point or range is largely defined by market forces. Those forces include investor and creditor expectations that interact around a variety of perceived trade-offs between risk and reward.

Liquidity

Of the four traditional PELL categories, only liquidity comes close to what we mean by cash flow. Most commonly, liquidity is evaluated by looking at the ratio of short-term assets to short-term liabilities, called the *current ratio*. If the short-term assets—primarily accounts receivable and inventory—exceed the short-term liabilities by a wide enough margin, there should be enough cash flowing in. Cash actually flows in only after conversion from inventory to sales, then on through receivables and back again to cash. At that point

> **The current ratio is rooted in the point-in-time values of the balance sheet and therefore says nothing about operational flows.**

it is used to pay suppliers, workers and other short-term obligations as they come due.

Unfortunately, the current-ratio approach to liquidity is limited, even though it does give some insight into the likely ability to meet obligations in the near term. To see that limitation clearly, consider that assets and liabilities are listed on the balance sheet in order of decreasing liquidity. Another way to think about the relative liquidity of different categories of assets and liabilities is to substitute the idea of *velocity*. The closer a category is to the top of the balance sheet, the quicker the turnover will be. Cash flows faster than receivables, which flow faster (usually) than inventory, equipment and real estate. Thus, the main limitation in assessing liquidity on a balance-sheet basis is that it has a static, point-in-time orientation; it completely fails to incorporate the operating perspective of the income statement. The current ratio is rooted in the point-in-time values of the balance sheet and therefore says nothing about operational flows. For that we must go to the cash-flow statement in the form of the UCA's cash-adjusted income statement described beginning on page 50.

Ratio Analysis

Ratio analysis is probably most helpful when it is used in time series across several accounting periods. It shows how management responds to a variety of conditions. It is not terribly helpful to learn, for example, that the current net-profit margin is 4.6% or that the current ratio (short-term assets divided by short-term liabilities) is 2.5. It is much more significant to see how these measures move over time—to see, for example, that leverage as measured by the debt-to-net-worth ratio moved gradually upward over a period of years. Further analysis reveals that this upward trend in leverage was accompanied by increased inventory and receivable days. As it turns out, these were needed to accommodate a broader product line and some shift in distribution channels. Movement and trends in ratios tell us much more than just a single number can because we can infer from such trends much about management's probable decision-making patterns.

Movement and trends in ratios tell us much more than just a single number can because we can infer from such trends much about management's probable decision-making patterns.

Another aspect of ratio analysis is what it may tell us preliminarily about likely cash-flow implications; the ratios suggest a certain type of cash-flow impact. The cash-flow statement then tests and quantifies that suggestion more specifically. For example, close inspection of Jones Dynamite Co.'s financials would show gradual deterioration of the current ratio from 2.2 to 1.8 over a three-year period and suggest declining liquidity—that is, a declining ability to pay current expenses from operating sources of cash. But when we look at the company's cash-flow statement, it shows a significantly positive and increasing net cash-income value over the same three-year period.

The question, then, is which better measures liquidity—the acceptable and improving operating-cash flow from the cash-flow statement, or the significantly declining current ratio rooted in the static data from the balance sheet? The static measure might be more useful if the company were in big trouble and facing liquidation. In fact, though, most of the time we deal not with issues of immediate liquidation but with questions of ongoing operational cashflowability. Our focus is primarily the going concern and how to keep it going as it continues to generate most of its own fuel from internal operating sources. Recall that the inability to do just that is what drove the once great W.T. Grant Co. into bankruptcy.

The Ultimate Cash-Flow Risk: Bankruptcy

When a business's cash flow continues to be too much out and not enough in, the result can be the need to file for formal bankruptcy. Chapter 11 bankruptcy is the *good news* of bankruptcy law. It is intended to create breathing space through temporary relief from creditors so that a business can reorganize itself and perhaps recover from its cash-flow failure—that is, begin to create enough positive cash flow to again pay debts as they come due. Inefficient operations can be closed down, needed layoffs instituted, nonessential assets sold at fair market value and debts restructured.

Under a sound Chapter 11 plan with good management, creditors are likely to be repaid at something near full value. In contrast, a forced liquidation under Chapter 7 bankruptcies will likely bring them only fire-sale values. But Chapter 11 is not available to everyone. It requires the agreement of creditors to an operating-cash-flow plan that is strong enough to persuade an appointed panel of those creditors to wait for things to get better. Management must convince the panel that the prospect of being paid something like full value in cash in the intermediate term is worth more than fractional repayment values in the somewhat shorter term. In the absence of confidence in a proposed cure, the plug is pulled and a Chapter 7 liquidation ensues. Under this plan, the frozen illiquid assets that had not produced adequate cash flow are involuntarily melted down, usually at considerable loss. They are liquified and dribbled out to creditors by a court-appointed trustee.

The Z Score: A Bankruptcy Early Warning System

The most important thing to learn about bankruptcy is how to avoid it. Careful management of the seven cash drivers that will be discussed in the following chapters will certainly help a company avoid bankruptcy. In addition, there is an early warning system for bankruptcy that is both easy to use and free of charge. It is called the Z-Score, and it is a useful number to track over time to see how your overall company risk level is moving. Because its calculation involves several of the ratios we have just reviewed, this is a particularly good time to look at it more closely. First, however, a few words of background.

The Z-Score was devised by Dr. Edward Altman at New York University's Stern School of Business. The database consisted of manufacturing companies, and the score incorporates a key ratio tied to the *market value* of equity. If your company is not manufacturing firm, the score less relevant. However, there is a school of thought that says risk is independent of the industry and, therefore, can be measured simply by analysis of profitability, efficiency, liquidity and leverage (PELL) ratios. Altman's Z-Score formula draws on all four of the ratio categories but also incorporates one particular ratio that uses market value of equity so that you need to come up with some realistic estimate of your own market value if you are not a publicly traded company.

Here's the formula for determining your Z-Score

Z = 1.2 x 1 + 1.4 x 2 + 3.3 x 3 + .6 x 4 + .999 x 5
X1 = Working capital ÷ Total assets
X2 = Retained earnings ÷ Total assets
X3 = Earnings before interest and taxes (EBIT) ÷ Total assets
X4 = Market value of equity ÷ Liabilities
X5 = Sales ÷ Total assets

Interpret a Z-Score of 3 or better as good. Consider scores between 1.8 and 2.9 as warning of potential problems. A score below 1.8 indicates major trouble and a likely descent into bankruptcy.

No matter where you find your company on this Z-Score

scale, an understanding of and attention to the seven cash drivers is the most effective improvement approach available.

Getting Ready for a Closer Look at the Cash Drivers

As we begin to look at the cash drivers one by one, remember that although these are not the *only* things that affect cash flow, they are the drivers. For most organizations, most of the time, changed measures in the levels of these drivers will account for nearly all of the variability in cash flow. The sequence in which we will discuss the drivers represents the most common pattern for relative importance. Sales growth, the subject of the next chapter, is the biggest single potential cash-flow driver overall. Gross margin and operating expense (SG&A) are considered fundamental drivers because they address the issues that a business's top management is paid to focus its energies on—the firm's production, buying, marketing and general management dimensions. Accounts receivable, inventory and accounts payable are considered swing drivers because regardless of what is happening at the level of the growth rate and fundamentals, the way these three are managed can swing the company's cash position positively or negatively. If, for example, the fundamentals are eroding, tighter management of the swing drivers can offset some of the negative impact of that erosion. Capital expenditures, the seventh driver, is almost always discretionary.

Increases in a swing driver's use of cash has both growth and relative dimensions. A higher sales level alone will tend to drive up dollars in the swing-driver accounts proportionally to sales or cost of goods sold in dollar terms. In addition, though, the choices by which management creates such a sales increase could also have the effect of changing the proportion. For example, say that top management decided to offer easier credit terms as a competitive marketing tool to bring in new customers. There would certainly be a proportional increase in receivables dollars resulting from the higher level of sales—the impact of growth. Receivables dollars would also increase because of the more liberal payment terms. This latter part of the increase would manifest itself by a jump in the relative measure of *days receivable*—the impact of the management decision.

You may wonder how seven items, the cash drivers, can have such a controlling effect on a firm. Consider for a moment what is involved. Sales growth, gross margin and operating expense have embedded in them most of the key dimensions of the operating part of the income statement. Receivables, inventory, payables and capital expenditures pick up the main operating controllables from the balance sheet. These drivers capture the core of the firm's financial statements and have embedded within them all of the company's key relationships with employees, customers and suppliers.

Armed with some background on cash flow, a brief overview of the cash drivers, a primer on basic accounting and a look at some of the cash-flow implications of traditional ratios analysis let's consider each cash driver individually in depth.

The Seven
Cash Drivers

Sales Growth:
The Dominant Driver

IGNIFICANT CASH-FLOW GROWTH ALMOST ALWAYS STARTS with sales growth. Maintaining or improving margins must be a high priority, and operating expense control is also a critical discipline. Tight control over the swing factors—receivables, inventory and payables—can make a substantial difference in cash flow. And certainly, strategically sound capital budgeting can affect both cashflowability and profitability for years to come. But it all starts with sales.

Increased sales have no upper limit, whereas margins, expense control, swing factor and capital budgeting are all limited to the particular sales-volume ballpark in which your business operates. Clearly, expanding the size of the ballpark is the most important single factor affecting cash flow and, therefore, the sum of all expected future cash flows. If we discount all those expected future cash flows back to today, we arrive at the current value of the firm. In many industries, there are rule-of-thumb valuation formulas, but such formulas are ultimately proxies for expectations as to discounted cash flows. In some ways, therefore, this chapter is not just about sales growth but about growth in a larger sense; ultimately, it is about growing the value of the firm. Having said that, though, I want to focus on sales growth as the critical first step in building the firm's total value. The total value of the enterprise is ultimately the discounted present value of all likely future cash flows—and those future cash flows all have to start with sales.

The present value of a business is the sum of all future cash flows discounted back to today. The negative interest rate we would apply to a company's future cash-flow projections is actually a risk-adjusted investment-return figure.

If you're not familiar with the idea of discounted cash flow, consider applying a *reverse compounded interest rate*. A reverse, or *negative* rate will reduce principal when applied to a positive value. For example, a $1,000, zero-coupon bond that's due to mature next year at its face value has a lower value today. Its present value is its future value a year out minus an amount equal to the going interest rate on that type of financial instrument. In the same way, the present value of a business is the sum of all future cash flows discounted back to today. The negative interest rate we would apply to a company's future cash-flow projections is actually a risk-adjusted investment-return figure. In Chapter 14 we'll discuss company valuation in depth, but the point for now is that in talking about sales growth, we are also talking in a parallel way about value growth.

As we briefly discussed in the previous chapter, there are two dimensions to the way sales growth affects cash flow—the growth effect itself and the management effect. Sales growth will naturally tend to have a somewhat proportional impact on virtually every other significant income-statement and balance-sheet line item. This occurs as rising sales figures ripple through the financial statements period by period. But management decisions about how to pursue and facilitate that growth, such as allowing customers easier credit terms or other changes to the marketing mix can have a substantial impact on cash flow, too. This challenges management to respond creatively to the operational issues involved in any significant growth.

Returning now to the purely proportional effects of sales growth, keep in mind that many line items and subtotals on the financial statements are likely to be affected. Balance-sheet changes are almost invariably driven by sales revenue. Changes in the income statement start at the first line—that is, revenue—and follow from there, generally in a somewhat proportional way. Finally, the cash-flow statement is affected as it is assembled from the integration of the balance sheets and income statement.

If growth consumes cash, is it not then logical to assume that negative growth, that is, a sales decline, can generate cash? Most of the time, this will prove to be true, as lower levels of assets are needed to keep the business running smoothly, albeit at a somewhat lower sales level. With lower sales rippling through the business, supporting assets can, therefore, be converted to cash. Most obviously, this applies to inventory and accounts receivable. Theoretically and ultimately, though, it applies to any class of asset and to most categories of expense.

Growth That Ripples

A shift in sales volume either upward or downward ripples through the company in a similar direction. Limits to responsiveness in sales-volume changes are based on what's called the *step-function* nature of many assets and costs. Step function refers to the fact that a lot of resources can be acquired or divested only in large chunks, or steps, bigger than may suit you at the moment. For example, a drop in sales volume necessarily cuts into your ability to pay for those fixed costs that don't automatically decline with drops in sales volume. Your landlord doesn't sympathetically take back 20% of the warehouse space you've been occupying and cut your rent proportionally just because you experience a 20% sales drop. The result is that it is relatively easy to have excess capacity in multiple aspects of your business at any given time. One saving grace, though, is that big fixed costs—that is, larger step functions—tend to be offset somewhat by large gross margins. Let's take a look at how margins and fixed costs tend to relate inversely to each other.

If you are in a high-fixed-cost business, the "growth takes cash" truism doesn't kick in very much until you approach capacity. This is due to the fact that gross margins are quite high. A motel, for example, would be typical of this high-fixed-cost kind of business. The direct cost of renting out one additional room is a very small fraction of the revenue one takes in from the guest, thus we see very high gross margins. On the other hand, on a busy holiday weekend in a resort area, you can't quickly, easily or inexpensively load up on an extra couple of dozen rooms to accommodate demand. Across the street, there's a restaurant that can extend its waiting line, open earlier, close later and place larger orders with its food and beverage wholesalers. Its gross margins, though, are a lot lower than yours. In the motel business, your slow season doesn't automatically bring with it reduced mortgage payments or taxes, your biggest costs. But in the slow midwinter, your friend the restaurateur's food, beverage and labor costs drop by 75%.

Take the time to get familiar with the cost structure of your industry and company. It can help liberate you from the tunnel vision that a preoccupation with your own function can sometimes force on you.

Take the time to get familiar with the cost structure of your industry and company. It will give you a real edge in understanding why things are the way they are and, more important, how they might be changed for the better. Understanding such financial structures will also help liberate you from the tunnel vision that a preoccupation with your own function can sometimes force on you. If your responsibility is sales or marketing, for example, an understanding of cash flow and the cash drivers should help you broaden your focus. This refocusing needs to go beyond straight sales volume and expand to include of pricing, selling-expense control and product-line breadth. Other things being equal, for example, it is often better to cut sales volume back a bit rather than to shave price just to get a few more deals. The particulars of that equation, though, depend on the specifics of cost, margin and step-function issues in your company and industry.

Marketing Mix
& the Management Effect

S ignificant sales growth does not just happen. It is generally planned and brought about through some deliberate
chain of analysis and decision making—what I call the
management effect. Those decisions are then implemented
and the result, hopefully, is sales growth. Think for a moment
of some of the things that typically create major sales growth:
new products, new markets, sales-force recruiting and training, new advertising and promotional campaigns, improved
service levels, changes in distribution-
channel strategy, and pricing. All these **Shifting your customer's**
possibilities are traditional elements of **perceptions about**
what is known as the *marketing mix*. **product and value**

Lots of planning and management **propositions can**
attention typically go into these market- **sometimes take years.**
ing-mix adjustment efforts, as Judy
Nagengast, CEO of Continental Design, can clearly attest. Her
plans for CD, a contract staffing firm in the midwest with a consistent record of 30% annual growth, started with sales growth,
but she has also concentrated on reengineering the marketing
mix in significant ways. New-product development is expensive,
as is entry into new markets. Changes in distribution channels
and selling methods can easily take several months or longer to
make; and then they have to be de-bugged and fine-tuned.
Shifting your customers' perceptions about product and value
propositions can sometimes take years.

Even relatively simple modifications to existing products,
along with associated repositioning or repricing efforts, are
often more complex, and even dangerous, than they may first
appear. One specialized software developer, Financial
Proformas Inc., in Walnut Creek, Cal., introduced a new version of an established, industry-leading product that was
already in its fifth generation. The new version was designed to
run with the latest IBM operating system; then Microsoft ran
away with the operating-system market for business PCs, and
the company saw sales volume drop precipitously. It took
Financial Proformas more than two nearly disastrous years to

regroup and catch up from the bad bet it had made by tying its main revenue source to IBM's OS2 platform.

This software-business example involved what looked like an adjustment rather than a major reengineering of the marketing mix, such as Judy Nagengast attempted at Continental Design. There, too, the conditions held high levels of technological risk.

Significant marketing-mix change in pursuit of major sales growth is almost always expensive. It is expensive in terms of both the additional assets and the direct expense levels that will inevitably be necessary.

Significant marketing-mix change in pursuit of major sales growth is usually expensive, in terms of both the additional assets and the direct-expense levels that will inevitably be necessary. The cash requirement doesn't stop with that up-front investment though. There is also the higher level of investment in inventory and accounts receivable to support the higher sales level. And there are increased cash requirements for the ongoing elements of marketing-mix adjustments that trickle down through the income statement. In most cases, they ripple into increased SG&A costs. Such increases become almost inevitable as a company becomes larger and more complex.

At Continental Design, the contract-engineering staffing business was in need of major marketing-mix changes to stay technologically current and meet shifting customer needs. In response, CD soon began to offer clients the services of contract engineers in tandem with the equipment they needed to do their work. CD staffers could arrive at the customer's job site fully outfitted and ready to go, with computer workstations, associated software and, of course, any necessary additional training. Clearly, this was a major shift in the marketing mix.

Around this same time, CD also began a closely related in-house service bureau for computer-assisted design. Product, people, pricing, training, capital investment and a shift in channel strategy all underwent major changes in a short period of time. The cash-flow planning it took to make all this happen was particularly critical. The increased up-front cash demands for all the mix changes that CD was planning posed a huge potential conflict with ongoing financing needs for maintaining or increasing its historic 30% sales-growth rate.

Judy Nagengast credits cash-flow planning and careful trade-offs among sometimes conflicting goals as an important key to CD's continued success. The company's annual financial plan has as its centerpiece a cash-flow projection that is prepared by an ex-banker who helps the company articulate and quantify its options and trade-offs. He demonstrated that the company's combination of rapid growth and mix-change plans threatened a cash drain. That risk and its likely impact on borrowing capacity had to be balanced against the additional debt needed to handle rapidly increasing capital-expenditure needs. Because the cash flow and strategic planning regarding these issues was done well in advance, the company was able to solve the problem, through a combination of very careful timing and presentation of a case that convinced lenders that a temporary spike in leverage would not significantly increase their risk of loss. A knowledgeable and deliberate plan, rather than a last-minute cash-flow panic, bolstered the firm's reputation, reduced operating stresses and allowed management to focus on true management issues rather than putting out the cash-flow fires that are often unwittingly set by managers who don't think in cash-driver terms.

Growth Takes Cash

I have made the point repeatedly that growth takes cash, and lots of growth takes lots of cash. For that reason, perhaps the only thing worse for a company than no growth is poorly planned-for growth. Such unplanned or poorly planned growth inevitably heightens the risk that unanticipated cash shortages will leave the enterprise stranded at the edge of the road, out of gas. Despite a growing emphasis in the business world on cash flow in general and its relationship to sales growth in particular, companies often tend to listen to the cash-flow words without hearing the cash-flow message. For many people in senior management, there is still an essential conflict between what they hear and what their gut tells them. Sales-volume growth has been so ingrained into entrepreneurs (as well it should be!) that it often combines with some simplistic, mostly erroneous logic to tell them something that is false, yet hard to ignore:

a) the company needs cash, therefore

b) sell lots of stuff, and

c) customers will give us money, and

d) the cash problem will go away

The reason this thought pattern is *mostly* rather than totally false is that it often works—but only in certain limited and relatively short-term situations. Yes, you can sell a few more items out of inventory without replacing them right away. Yes, you can negotiate earlier payment terms with a couple of clients on specific orders. Yes, you can negotiate extended terms with one or two suppliers for a specified project or purpose. Yes, in an emergency you can get your plant to close for two weeks in a slow season for a cash-conserving companywide vacation. But you cannot do any, much less all, of these things consistently, across the board, without creating long-term stress fractures in your business.

At the same time that new directions and resources are taking form and being put into motion to increase sales growth, all of the more routine elements of the business's existing operations have to continue smoothly. And that continuance will likely involve a lot of additional pressure on your people, your organizational structures and your finances. As you gear up to grow rapidly and prepare to digest that growth, a whole lot can go wrong. There is also an interdependence among all those pieces that can easily get bent out of shape under the increased pressure.

Occasionally a business gets lucky and, due to fortuitous circumstances, manages to avoid much of the hard work and good planning normally required for generating significant sales growth. This is usually a matter of just being in the right place at the right time as the market comes to you. Here are several examples.

■ **A medium-size natural-foods wholesaler** happened to have a well-known expert on natural foods move to its community and take a personal interest in spreading the natural-foods mes-

sage throughout the area the wholesaler served.
- ■ **A small chain of upscale shoe stores** had major new luxury-housing developments built in three of its five markets over a two-year period.
- ■ **A large ornamental ironworks shop** saw its business triple in three years because of the influence of a talented interior designer who specified a lot of wrought iron in several new commercial buildings.

But, as the saying goes, don't hold your breath. This kind of good luck doesn't happen very often and can't be predicted or relied on. Ironically, lucky scenarios such as these can be *bad* luck if the growth is not managed well. These cases didn't require planning to create additional demand; that is the good luck part. But some planning was definitely required to handle the financial, people and other kinds of resource strains that such growth normally triggers.

Any growth beyond what is sustainable in cash terms will cause financial problems every time. Well, almost every time. There is one exception: excess assets. If a company has more inventory than it needs to keep things running smoothly, then additional sales volume doesn't take cash; it simply uses up excess inventory. Having any asset that either isn't needed, or isn't needed in the current quantity to keep the business running smoothly, is a cash-conversion opportunity. A company can sell any excess asset, then use the cash to finance growth beyond what is otherwise sustainable from just cash profits and proportional debt increases. The key here is that management needs to know within a fairly tight range just what rate of sales growth can actually be sustained, given normal cash profit and debt-percentage levels. If management doesn't have a sense of that range, it will likely target sales levels either lower than are optimally achievable or higher than are healthily sustainable. There is an optimal growth rate, and management needs to focus on it. If overall proportions of debt and equity in the business are about what they should be, and if both the fundamentals and the swing factors are stable, then calculating the sustainable growth rate is fairly easy, as we will discuss later in this chapter.

Breakeven Analysis & Contribution Margin

One of the easiest ways to demonstrate the linkage between sales growth and its propensity to absorb rather than generate cash is to do some traditional *breakeven analysis*, then to examine how that analysis has to be modified for growth's associated cash impacts. Let's begin with a definition of breakeven: It is the point at which total expenses and total revenues are equal. There is neither profit nor loss. At this point, gross margins are exactly offset by the sum of operating costs and any financing expenses. There is no income-tax expense at the breakeven point because there is no profit.

An important distinction in breakeven analysis is that between *fixed costs* and *variable costs*. Fixed costs are those that stay about the same regardless of how much product is sold. Examples are rent, most utilities and salaries, depreciation, and long-term financing costs. Variable costs, as the term implies, vary directly with sales volume. Examples include direct product costs, sales commissions and delivery expenses.

An important term in breakeven analysis is *contribution margin*—that is, how much is available out of each sales dollar to contribute to covering fixed costs and profit. At Jones Dynamite Co., variable costs accounted for approximately 40% of their selling price for the avarage product. That means that 60 cents of the typical sales dollar was available to contribute to coverage of fixed costs and profit. Breakeven analysis calculates the sales volume required for total company revenue to exactly cover all costs. The formula is:

Dollars of total fixed cost ÷ Contribution margin as a decimal

In Jones's case, total fixed cost was $4,246,800 and contribution margin was .60. Dividing the former by the latter yields a breakeven sales volume of $7,078,000. Any sales-volume figure below this value would have caused Jones to show a loss, and anything above it a profit. For the next year, Jones was forecasting a 14% increase in fixed costs to handle some anticipated sales-growth opportunities. To calculate the new breakeven point, we first multiply last year's fixed costs by the anticipated increase (in this case, 14%, or 1.14), then divide by the contribution margin, which was expected to remain at the same .60. The formula is: last year's fixed expenses times one plus the increase fixed-cost percentage, divided by contribution margin equals breakeven point, or

$$\$4,246,800 \times 1.14 \div .60 = \$8,068,920$$

The new forecasted breakeven sales level rose by $990,920. But that is only on an accrual basis; it gives no consideration to the additional cash investments in accounts receivable and inventory that will almost certainly be required to support the higher sales level. This remains true even after netting out some offsetting increases in accounts-payable support by suppliers. Let's quickly estimate what those needed cash increases will likely be.

At the end of last year the total of all accounts receivable plus all inventory, minus all accounts payable came to $1,245,888. Remember, we are assuming no change in the *relative levels* of receivables, inventory, payables or gross margins—therefore, the expected increase in these items will be equal to the percentage increase in sales volume.

Applying the new 14% higher breakeven-point figure to last year's net dollar value of Jones's receivables, inventory and accounts payable yields a negative cash effect of $174,424. The point here is that the sales increase required to cover the new, higher level of fixed costs on a supposedly breakeven basis still comes up nearly $175,000 short in cash terms. Growth takes cash, and lots of growth takes lots of cash because cash is the fuel on which the enterprise runs. And just as with most of life, the faster you go, the faster you burn the fuel.

A faster fuel-burn rate can mean either, or both, of two things. Certainly, the faster you go, the faster you run out of fuel. It can also mean, though, that the faster you go, the less efficiently you burn the fuel. As the sales-growth rate rises, newer, less-experienced people are frequently hired, and older, less-efficient equipment is often put back into service.

Administrative and support systems risk becoming over-stressed, and flows of information tend to become garbled more easily. Decision-making quality sometimes suffers as the merely urgent pushes the truly important to the back burner.

Rapid growth puts pressure on your financial structures and tends to push leverage ratios into more risky territory, such that lenders' expectations often begin to play a larger role in your decision making. And, of course, the more your lenders are in control, the less your stockholders will like it.

In addition to these process-efficiency risks, rapid growth also puts pressure on your financial structures and tends to push leverage ratios into more risky territory, such that lenders' expectations often begin to play a larger role in your decision making. And, of course, the more your lenders are in control, the less your stockholders will like it. Clearly, the best growth is planned growth, as we saw at Continental Design. But what constitutes the *right* growth rate around which to plan? It should now be clear that *all-you-can-sell* is the wrong answer, unless *all-you-can-sell* represents a pretty trivial growth rate. I have used the term *sustainable* with respect to growth several times. Now it's time to come back to it and examine it in some detail. Then I will demonstrate how to calculate sustainability and show why it may represent the ideal sales-growth target for most firms.

Sustainable Sales Growth

We keep coming back to a basic observation about sales growth: It is very often a mixed blessing and must be managed carefully. You cannot afford to push sales uncritically for volume—not even for profitable volume. You must first pay careful attention to the cash effects of your growth rate. Growth takes cash and there is a balance point for growth, a point of cash-flow sustainability at which an organization can continue to grow indefinitely. And so, for sustainability, you will want to depend for fuel on a combination of your own internally generated cash, plus just enough additional debt to keep things in the same financing proportions.

If financing proportions get out of whack—with much more debt, for example—risk goes up. Interest as an expense factor would probably go up even more, and your suppliers might begin to manage their receivables just a bit more tightly because of the heightened perception of risk. This, in turn, may constrain the depth and breadth of your inventory enough to disrupt merchandising or production. One further result is some likely erosion of margins. Maintaining your financing proportions may prevent that significant risk-factor spiral from developing. All this is *not* to say that current financing proportions and leverage measures are automatically optimal. Determining the optimal degree of leverage goes beyond the scope of this book. We will simply assume that your current capital structure is about what it should be. We will make our calculation of sustainable growth, therefore, with the assumption of no change in measures of leverage.

Growth takes cash and there is a balance point for growth, a point of cash-flow sustainability, at which an organization can continue to grow indefinitely.

In addition to a constant debt-to-equity ratio, the sustainable-growth concept and its calculation are centered in two other core assumptions: that you are able to hold the line on the proportion of your profit retained for investment in your business, and that there is no change in the marketing efficiency of assets as measured by the ratio of assets to sales. The traditional formula for sustainable growth that results from these assumptions is designed to answer a very specific question, that is, assuming that you don't change the current debt-to-equity ratio and that you are able to maintain the current level of sales-to-assets efficiency: What level of sales growth will the net-profit margins that are retained in the business be able to support?

To be sure you grasp the importance of sustainable growth, I want to restate it in slightly different terms: Sustainable growth represents a balanced steady-state business. It is balanced in the sense that the company's growth rate causes it to generate exactly the right amounts of additional internal and external cash—just enough to fund the extra assets and expenses required to achieve the growth actually experienced. It is steady-state in that:

- **its efficiency of asset use in creating sales** remains unchanged;
- **its efficiency in operations, financing and taxation** leaves net profit margins unchanged; and
- **the percentage of earnings paid out as dividends** remains unchanged.

In other words, a sustainable growth rate is one that maintains balanced steady-state growth without creating either a cash shortage or a cash surplus. The cash balances or money supply of the firm remain in the same proportion to sales, assets and expenses.

Managing Sustainability

Growing faster than allowed by the sustainable rate will require more cash than the steady-state scenario can generate. That extra cash has to come from somewhere, and the options (as we have already seen) are limited to:

- **reducing the percentage of profit paid out in dividends,** thus conserving cash;
- **borrowing proportionally more than in the past**—that is, increasing the debt-to-equity ratio, thereby providing cash;
- **increasing net margins by reducing unit costs,** getting more economies of scale on overhead expenses, or getting price increases that stick—all cash generators; and
- **improving asset efficiency**—that is, increasing assets at a rate slower than sales growth. This, too, yields positive cash flows.

In short, when it comes to sustainable growth, as the song says, something's got to give.

Let's now look at the sustainable-growth formula. It is surprisingly simple:

Net income ÷ (Net worth − Net income) = Sustainable growth

For Jones Dynamite Co. last year, this was:

$$\$508,200. \div (\$3,388,000 - \$508,200) = 17.6\%$$

As with most firms, Jones's proportional relationship between sales and its various asset categories doesn't vary much from year to year. Also, as with most small companies, Jones doesn't pay out any of its earnings in dividends, nor does it expect to do so anytime soon. The business has nothing in its plans that would likely cause significant shifts in its gross margins or operating-expense ratios. Interest and tax costs will likely remain proportionally very close to last year's figures as well. The relative mix of profit going to retained earnings should remain unchanged, and any additional liabilities in the form of payables, accruals, or actual cash borrowings will stay in the same proportions, according to Jones's controller. Under these conditions, the sustainable-growth formula says that Jones is limited by cash resources to about 17.6% sales growth in the coming year unless it can find some new fuel sources. That's how much growth can be absorbed or financed by the combination of internally generated cash flow, and just enough in the way of additional liabilities to keep the debt-to-equity ratio from rising.

Bear in mind that this sustainable-growth formula is operating on a basis of accrual profit. It does *not*, therefore, take into account *cash* profit level, but only reported accounting profit. As we saw earlier in the discussion of rule-of-thumb cash flow, cash and accrual results will be the same only under the kind of absolute stability represented by the constancy assumption in all the relevant areas—net margins retained, debt-to-equity ratio and sales-to-assets efficiency. Actual sustainable growth will fall below the calculated value if any of those key variables should drop in the coming period. Conversely, sustainable-growth potential for the coming period will go up as leverage, net margins retained, or sales-to-assets efficiency measures increase. To put it another way, you can increase your sustainable growth rate if you:

■ **put proportionally more debt on your balance sheet** without undue costs;

■ cut operating-cost ratios, tax rates, or interest rates on debt;
■ raise prices without incurring either offsetting cost increases or drops in sales volume;
■ cut the percentage of earnings paid out in dividends; or
■ squeeze proportionally more sales out of your present asset base.

Note that this discussion of sustainable growth implicitly assumes that the only increases in your equity are from profit retained in the business. For some small companies, this may have to be the case. For most firms, however, additional equity *is* obtainable on some reasonable basis. Most basic would be an investment your family might come up with, or a second mortgage on your home. Other options include business and professional people who have confidence in you and your business potential. Or you could bring in one or more active partners who have some significant abilities to add value to the business, beyond just their capital contributions, or merge with a business that has a better balance between growth and cash flow than yours does. This last option, the business combination, is presented in some detail in the next section of this chapter. It deserves separate treatment because it represents a very specialized case of sales growth and is of potentially enormous impact. Also, it has some important cash-flow dimensions that are often badly misunderstood.

Finding financial angels, seeking venture capitalists and going public round out the remaining equity choices. The question of which equity sources might be most appropriate to your situation is beyond the scope of this book. (*Raising Capital*, by Andrew Sherman, another book in Kiplinger's Business Management Library, would be a good source for information on this issue.) Rather, I intend simply to alert you to the equity-expansion issue you will have to deal with in considering any growth beyond the sustainable. This turns attention to the question of the cost of equity relative to the cost of capital. While I won't be covering that topic directly, I will discuss some elements of equity and capital cost in the context of valuing the business in Chapter 14.

It should be clear that senior management needs to focus continually on seeking out new options—the kind that can permanently escalate sustainable growth to higher levels of equilibrium. A closely related responsibility is to keep *actual* growth rates pushing right up to the sustainable targets. And here everyone in the company must keep that process by getting more mileage out of every dollar of both assets and expense, while at the same time creating more value in both real and perceived terms for your customers. An understanding of cash-flow dynamics and reasonable mastery of cash-driver language will help make these objectives realistic.

Senior management needs to focus continually on seeking out new options— the kind that can permanently escalate sustainable growth to higher levels of equilibrium. A closely related responsibility is to keep *actual* growth rates pushing right up to the sustainable targets.

Big-Gulp Sales Growth & Cash-Flow Implications

This section, which might be subtitled *Way Beyond Sustainability*, covers two special cases. (A third case, involving the issuance of new equity, will not be covered because I have no particular insight to offer, nor do I see any particularly unique cash-flow dimension to that option.) These are where potential sales growth involves redoing the balance sheet starting with the net-worth section:

- conserving equity by elimination of excess payments to owners; and
- combining equity by merger or acquisition.

The two cases are actually more similar than they are different. For that reason I will cover them on an integrated basis. In each case there is a question about the relative value and utility of the firm's equity—how it is best used. In the case of dividends or other payments to owners, the question is whether the owners are better off with taxable cash returns or a tax-free reinvestment in the business's growth prospects. In the case of potential mergers or acquisitions, the question is similar: Are the owners better off with a total interest in the company as it is, on a stand-alone basis, or with an equitable *partial* interest in a combined *new* firm with higher sustainable-growth potentials relative to their cost? Remember here, too, the opening point of the chapter—that is, the function that cash flow serves as a proxy for measuring a company's growth in value.

Paying out a dividend or excessive income to owners is often an unintended economic acknowledgement by management that it doesn't have the creativity to use the cash wisely in the business.

Sometimes the dividend and merger cases blend together, as in situations where the elimination of dividends frees up cash to fund smaller acquisitions. In all of these situations, though, maximization of owners' value will be determined by the net present value of all the future cash flows likely to be associated with each choice. Other things being equal, this will be shaped by the choice that provides the most sustainable-growth value for the investment dollar.

CONSERVING EQUITY BY ELIMINATION OF EXCESS PAYMENTS TO OWNERS

Paying out a dividend or excessive income to owners is often an unintended economic acknowledgment by management that it doesn't have the creativity to use the cash wisely in the business. This is why it is returned to shareholders to be spent, which can sometimes be a reasonable personal choice, or invested elsewhere through the hands of more creative management teams at other companies. If the latter is the case, why shouldn't a shareholder bail out of the dividend-paying investment in the first company altogether and put the proceeds into other solid nondividend-paying companies? Well-chosen acquisitions would almost always be a better choice for using cash than would paying out dividends once it is determined that enough high-yielding internal-investment opportunities can't be found. It is the relatively rare company that can't find good internal-investment opportunities if it takes the time and trouble to look. This is probably more true today than ever. Opportunities have multiplied enormously as a consequence of technology, consolidation, demographics, confidence, productivity and the vigor of the market system spreading more broadly across the globe.

One risk of adopting a policy of eliminating stockholder payouts is the temptation to overpay for acquisitions or expansions. The solution here is to undertake only those investments heavily enough leveraged to require managers' breaking a real sweat to pay the associated debt before their leveraged bonuses or stock options can build any significant value. Then, and only then, can there be reasonable assurance that you have not overpaid. Finally, if there are no good internal uses for the cash, and if there are no acquisitions that make economic sense, you still can buy back your own stock before paying dividends. By buying back a larger interest in your company from partners or family members or on the open market, you will at the very least ensure that only stockholders choosing to sell their shares will be taxed. In the case of dividends, management makes that usually suboptimal choice for the stockholders.

It is the relatively rare company that can't find good internal-investment opportunities if it takes the time and trouble to look.

COMBINING EQUITY BY MERGER OR ACQUISITION

Far below the level of Wall Street and the big publicly traded corporations, mergers and acquisitions are becoming a part of the evolutionary development of small and medium-size businesses. The more efficient absorb the less efficient. The more visionary absorb the less visionary. Perhaps the most important point of focus for smaller firms considering a business combination is to look for complementary strengths in their potential partners. This will allow them to leverage themselves by shoring up each other's weaknesses and playing off each other's strengths. The nature of the particular strengths and weaknesses to be leveraged or minimized are not terribly relevant overall, so long as they represent significant issues for the players within their environments.

Anything that can ratchet up your sales growth, improve competitive advantage in terms of price or margins, extend economies of scale, or enhance risk-adjusted returns by either more efficient asset utilization or better debt-to-equity structuring, can be a reason to seek out merger or acquisition opportunities. Not surprisingly, these benefits correspond almost directly to the cash drivers.

For smaller enterprises especially, management-succession issues can be particularly important as grounds for considering mergers. Often, subsequent generations of a family may follow other career directions yet still want to maximize the value of their interest in the family enterprise. One underutilized tactic that can help with cash-conserving succession planning is the ESOP—employee stock ownership plan. This permits some real latitude in structuring ownership shifts without loss of control or negative tax consequences. It can also blend well into a merger or acquisition plan.

> **Anything that can ratchet up your sales growth, improve competitive advantage in terms of price or margins, extend economies of scale, or enhance risk-adjusted returns by either more efficient asset utilization or better debt-to-equity structuring, can be a reason to seek out merger or acquisition opportunities.**

A variation on the traditional merger is called the roll-up. Here, several owners of smaller companies in a particular field pool some of their common resources but maintain their own operating identities. I recently came across an old friend doing just this in the consumer-catalog business. All the back office, computer, financial and fulfillment operations of several companies, including a shared ten-acre warehouse building, are rolled up—that is, commonly owned and managed. The unique identity, brand, product mix, merchandising strategies and mailing lists of the individual catalog operators remain intact as separate divisions in the new combined company. The hope is to create something big enough, and with a high enough overall sustainable-growth rate to be able to take the combined firm public. This holds promise for the owners of a valuation package far greater proportionally than any one of them could have achieved individually.

The ability to make such a plan work is driven by genuine economies of scale combined with the best of entrepreneurial market savvy. That combination is then rolled together and packaged into a total entity that is big enough to at least get within striking distance of the radar screens of mutual funds and other institutional-investment buyers. Left alone without their roll-up partners, the individual companies would probably never be able to achieve the necessary profitability, magnitude and visibility.

Often managements in companies both large and small look at potential acquisitions the same way they look at payments to owners. They act as though the primary issue is stock price or perceived company value, when in reality valuation is a consequence, not a cause, of good company economics. The focus on manipulating payments to owners to manage share prices in the market, or perceived value in private companies, is something of an insult to the soundness of the market and/or the other owners. Smart investors will see through such camouflage.

Most companies automatically eliminate from the field of acquisition candidates any company with a price-earnings ratio higher than their own. But the real issue is whether the two companies' coming together makes sense at the fundamental economic level of enhanced combined net present-value of future cash flows.

Most companies automatically eliminate from the field of acquisition candidates any company with a price-earnings ratio higher than their own. Like the payment of dividends, this is a counterproductive piece of conventional wisdom that relies more on belief than on demonstrable logic with supporting data. The real issue is whether the two companies' coming together makes sense at the fundamental economic level—whether it enhances the combined net present value of future cash flows. If so, what difference does the relative size of each company's Monopoly-money share certificates make? Whenever one company acquires another for stock, the P/E ratio of the new company will change. It will migrate to a level representing the average of the two individual P/Es weighted by their relative earnings. Stated another way, the value of the combined company will be the same as the sum of the two companies prior to the acquisition. The big exception to this is when the marketplace judges that the combined entity has net present values of expected cash flows that are either more or less than the sum of the original parts.

It makes little economic difference whether the marketplace in question is a stock exchange or simply your partners and family. In most merger or acquisition cases, there is some complementary strength between the entities. Almost always, it is a strength that affects at the cash-driver level and creates enhanced future cash flows based on the combination. The problem in acquiring a company whose P/E is higher than one's own for stock is not a real problem. The belief that it *is* a problem reflects biases that are rooted either in a failure to understand economic realities or in a management-compensation system tied to earnings per share instead of to real value creation. What if your business isn't publicly held, nor is merger or acquisition a direction you are likely to pursue? Why should you care about such things? The answer is found in your own desire that your company grow and prosper in other ways, because the same principles still apply.

> **In most merger or acquisition cases, there is some complementary strength between the entities. Almost always, it is a strength that affects at the cash-driver level and creates enhanced future cash flows based on the combination.**

If your plans for sales growth are more than sustainable, then to raise the level of growth that can be sustained, you have to acquire something you don't presently have. Maybe it is not another company, but perhaps it's a higher level of management expertise, or some pricey equipment or a new building. The point is that you will not be able to increase growth rate, profit and cash flow without the necessary investment. And making such investments will almost certainly cut into current profit and cash flow. Despite the earnings drop, though, your company's economic value *will* have increased. The amount of the increase will equal the net present value of the additional future cash flows those investments will likely yield in excess of any drop in near-term cash earnings. Depending on how you currently distribute profits, you may or may not be willing to take a current hit to profit and cash flow in exchange for greater future values. You are then doing the same kind of analysis and trade-offs as the management of the big publicly held company. This is so even in the context of price-earnings valuation, as we shall see.

You don't have to be a publicly held and actively traded company to be interested in the multiple of earnings at which your company is valued. Say, for example, that your company netted $100,000 after taxes last year and for management-succession reasons you are considering merging with a complementary business that netted the same. The question arises as to how ownership in the combined company should be split. At first glance, maybe 50/50 feels right until you remember that you have more in the way of tangible assets, mostly because you own the land and buildings in which your business is housed while your prospective merger partner leases. On that basis, you lean toward a 60/40 ownership split in your favor. But your suitor points out that his firm has been growing at double your growth rate for the past several years. This more than offsets the value of the real estate assets that you thought gave you such an edge. Finally you settle on 60/40 in his favor. Given that you have identical earnings, a 60/40 split in the ownership of the new combined company means that your partner's company was valued at a 50 percent higher P/E ratio than yours.

Since your earnings have been the same but your partner has been growing much faster, presumably that faster growth will produce a deeper, wider, faster cash-flow stream into the future and thereby justify the higher relative valuation.

Finally the deal is done. You have completed your merger, you have taken the ultimate "big gulp" of sales growth, and you need to begin working again on the other six cash drivers for the new combined entity. If you are still paying dividends, you may want to drop them if at all possible. This will free some cash for increasing the new combined sustainable-growth rate. Generally speaking, the best place to focus next is at your gross margin line, the next biggest positive number on the income statement. And you can attack that line from both the production-cost and selling-price sides of the equation. In a merchandising business you may have no production costs per se, but you do have possibilities for improvement in purchasing management. And, of course, price adjustments in selling your goods and services are also an option as you consider how to improve margins. Let's now consider those gross margins in some detail.

Gross Margin: First of the Fundamentals

ROSS MARGIN IS SALES MINUS THE DIRECT COST OF the product or service, which on the income statement is usually called cost of goods sold or cost of revenue. Sometimes, in a straight service business, though you might not use the same terminology you might list service-cost elements along with all the other operating-cost categories. Whenever possible, though, it is usually best to break out the specific cost of providing services separately from selling, general and administrative (SG&A) expenses. This is particularly important when there are meaningful distinctions in selling price and cost structure from one product, service type or cost element to another.

Gross margin in manufacturing, wholesaling and retailing is a particularly critical point of focus. First of all, it is what's available to cover all operating overhead, financing costs and income taxes, as well as any distribution to owners. It had better be sufficient. One way of helping to ensure sufficiency is to design your motivation and measurement systems so that they support the goal of maximizing gross-margin dollars.

There is an old adage that says you get what you measure. If you measure sales volume as the primary determinant of marketing success and as the basis on which to set marketing-related budgets, guess what? Sales will probably go up. But actually, increased sales volume isn't what you want. A higher gross margin is what you really want. If everyone involved in your sales and marketing would internalize that lesson and focus on its implications for both profit and cash flow, chances are you would get what you really want instead of just raw sales volume. Your managers should consider

Different products have different levels of margin. That reality needs to be reflected in product-management budgets as well as the commission and advertising plans.

applying commission rates or ad-budget percentages against dollars of targeted gross margin instead of against sales volume. Susan McCloskey understands this; she markets nearly $5 million in mostly refurbished furniture each year through the company she heads, Office Plan Inc., in St. Paul, Minn. And the sales force commission structure is geared not to sales volume at all, but directly to dollars of gross margin.

The same principle of measuring and rewarding what you are trying to achieve holds true when you look at product mix. Different products have different levels of margin. That reality needs to be reflected in product-management budgets as well as in the commission and advertising plans. Maybe there are also implications for product-mix optimization in package-pricing deals, or alternative delivery methods, or a variety of other options. And at some point, you may have to consider simply walking away from some lower-margin products or customers, or at least put a priority on starting to find replacements for the volume they represent.

The Two Sides of Margins

With gross margin, raising price is one side of the equation; reducing cost is the other. Improvements on either side of the equation increase gross margin. Different order quantities and discounts can be analyzed and negotiated to bring materials cost down. Long-term exclusive contracts with fewer and more reliable suppliers may save not only money but space as well. This works well when the supplier will warehouse parts or materials and ship to you in smaller quantities as needed. Decide what you want to achieve and put it out for proposal or bid. If you have a manufacturing operation, for example, consider the elements of your product in terms of a possible redesign. That may permit reductions in the number of manufacturing steps or the number of parts; also consider subcontracting out low-skill elements to others with lower cost structures.

As you consider possible price changes, try centering the analysis on identifying a new equilibrium where opportunities for the spread between total costs and total revenues are appreciably greater than at present.

All of these approaches can add to margin and can be accomplished either as part of an overall redesign project or incrementally. Little by little, sharp owners, partners, managers and supervisors paying close attention to the business elements nearest their daily tasks can make a significant difference in these areas. And cumulatively through them, increase the company's value. That kind of enhancement takes not only an understanding of the impact of the seven cash drivers, but also considerable discipline and time. Following through with the necessary communication and action takes plenty of effort.

On the price side of gross margin, you have presumably already set pricing strategy and policies that represent some kind of equilibrium point relative to your markets. As you consider possible price changes, try centering the analysis on identifying a new equilibrium where opportunities for the spread between total costs and total revenues are appreciably greater than at present. Later in the chapter we'll discuss pricing issues relative to distribution-channel strategy. First, we'll deal with setting a new price within an existing channel. There are three basic ways to accomplish this:

- **identifying and moving toward the product or service value already perceived by the customer;**
- **improving communication of your value message; and**
- **creating incremental value in both real and perceptual terms.**

Though any of these tactics may be the point of origin for repricing, usually you need to give consideration to all three.

As with any decision, the incremental costs and revenues need to be accurately estimated in each case. A bad pricing decision is often harder to reverse or remedy than other missteps, so accurate estimates become even more important.

The first tactic for repricing focuses on the appropriateness of current pricing— that is, the market's perception of the value of your goods or services.

The first tactic for repricing focuses on the appropriateness of current pricing— that is, the market's perception of the value of your goods or services. It may be that some reasonable level of price increase would be generally acceptable in your market without any particular need for elements of the second or third tactics.

The second tactic, improving communication of your own value message, may be very expensive, and nearly impossible in the extreme case of product that is nearly identical to its competitors, where there is little rationale for vendor loyalty. On the other hand, a highly differentiated product that is important to buyers would seem to have significant upside pricing potential—probably in proportion to how clearly customers understand and value the points of product differentiation you are trying to convey.

Finally, the third tactic, value creation, generally incorporates elements of the first two in addition to redesign of the product, service, maintenance, follow-up and ancillary aspects of the business. Some of these can be enormously expensive and others somewhat trivial.

Pricing is important enough that the results, or answers, surrounding all three tasks need to be periodically updated and reviewed in light of competitive, technological and macroeconomic events as well as customer perceptions.

Gross Margin & Contribution Margin

As important as gross margins are, they can conceal a lot of important information if not dealt with on a product-by-product or customer-by-customer basis. Aggregates often hide useful distinctions. On average, the Jones Dynamite

Co. has a gross margin of 65%, but the gross margins on its individual products and services range from 18% to 77%. Not only do gross margins vary widely, but so do contribution margins. Recall that contribution analysis separates all costs into either fixed or variable. It then calculates a contribution margin, that is, how much of every sales dollar is available to help cover— that is, *contribute to*—fixed costs and profit. Knowing what gross margins *and* contribution margins are on both a product and customer basis can improve overall margins by positioning you to take specific action where needed. That knowledge also helps you avoid coming up with overly broad solutions that affect products or customers that need no particular action or adjustment. Consider this example for two of Jones's 16 product lines:

	PRODUCT LINE A	PRODUCT LINE B
Revenue	$78,000	$56,000
Purchase or service cost	$33,250	$16,800
Gross margin	$44,750	$39,200
Gross margin %	56.8%	70.0%
Variable selling cost	$11,200	$13,850
Variable administrative cost	$1,550	$1,750
Contribution margin	$32,000	$23,600
Contribution margin %	41.0%	42.1%

Based on gross-margin percentage, product line B is the clear winner, but when contribution margin is calculated the two lines are virtually identical. If you were looking at gross margins alone, some bad decisions could easily be made.

If there are good business reasons, and there usually are, there is nothing wrong with having different levels of gross margins for different products. What is wrong is to assume that higher gross margins are inherently more profitable without first considering other elements of cost. Addressing the full cost issue is what contribution margin as illustrated in this Jones Dynamite example is all about. Suppose, for example, that based on gross-margin percentages of 70% vs. 56% for products A and B above, Jones decided to make some significant price concessions on product B for customers who buy B over A in a ratio of 2 to 1 or more. Without the above contribution-margin analysis, this decision could wipe out the majority of true customer profit. This is quite different from the intent, which was to gain some competitive insulation from cut-rate offers that a new supplier is starting to offer to some of Jones's best customers. Jones will indeed get the insulation but at a cost far higher than anticipated.

Refining Gross-Margin Calculations

Jones, in the preceding example, is a wholesaler and retailer. The issues get even more complicated in a manufacturing environment because there are so many more aspects and categories of costs that mount up as a product moves through a complex manufacturing process. Further rationalizing of those cost analyses and margin calculations can be nearly impossible without the use of a system that is designed to help you keep accurate track of the true costs of each step for each job or product. Fortunately, such activity-based costing (ABC) systems are readily available to track and assign costs accurately.

In plants that manufacture only a few similar products, having a single basis rate on which to allocate overhead costs makes sense. Most commonly that basis is labor hours because traditionally that has been the biggest cost element. The greater the number of different products and the greater your manufacturing complexity, the more likely it is that an ABC system will be a worthwhile investment. The conversion to an ABC system is a big project but one that will help reveal many unsound pricing and other decisions that are currently being masked by simplistic assumptions about assignment of factory overhead costs.

In a more complex environment, with more manufacturing steps, more departments and more products, overhead cost allocation should probably be broken out by each activity involved. ABC systems are really necessary in such cases, where labor rates may vary widely from one department to the next, and the relative mix of inputs may also vary by department. So in a hypothetical plant, department A may be highly labor-intensive with relatively highly paid specialists. Department B may also be labor intensive but employ much lower-cost general factory labor. Department C, by contrast, may be highly automated with minimal labor. Clearly, labor hours alone are the wrong way to allocate overhead costs in this plant.

If you are using gross margins as a cash driver, you must have confidence that the figures you use in making decisions are reasonable approximations of economic reality. If they are not, the errors will undoubtedly produce significant negative cash-flow effects.

In the most complex manufacturing situations, with many different products, activity-based costing is necessary to develop detailed cost-estimation processes for each activity in each department of the plant. It is important to get this kind of information right because if you are using gross margins as a cash driver, you must have confidence that the figures you use in making decisions are reasonable approximations of economic reality. If they are not, the errors will undoubtedly produce significant negative cash-flow effects.

While activity-based costing is of primary importance in accurately determining gross margins in a manufacturing environment, management of purchasing and inventory is usually the key in merchandising businesses, whether retail or wholesale. Timing, a sense of the market, the use of hedging, and knowing when to take markdowns are core issues for maintaining gross margins.

A key to success here revolves around the availability of the right information at the right time in the right form. Pay attention to the design and use of the reports that your accounting, finance and information-technology departments issue. Which ones really get used and by whom? On what do the reports and their readers focus and why? What do the relevant decision makers most want to know, and when? How can you get better information, sooner, in the most usable form, to the right people? Even partial reasonable answers to such questions will put your company on the road to higher gross margin. At the most basic level, anyone can contribute in this informational way. Begin simply by taking the time to study and more fully understand the content and implications of everyday reports as they exist. Pass your insights about this information along in writing to those who can best use it, and be willing to let them take, or at least share, the credit.

As you analyze your business from a gross-margin perspective, consider both the marketing and the production (or purchasing) sides of the firm. If you see a trend of decline in gross margins, it probably means that your company is a *price taker*—that it does not have sufficient power in the marketplace to be able to raise prices enough to cover all cost increases. Alternatively, a downward trend in gross margin when the same margin-erosion problem is not being experienced by the overall industry usually suggests production inefficiencies or poor buying patterns.

Additional value-creation opportunities abound in most companies. The trick is to motivate and empower people to act on them at their individual levels of influence. Equipping people with cash-driver language is an important early step in that direction.

If you work in production, production planning, purchasing or product development, be alert for those things that will add value for your customers. Improvements in perceived value can help to hold the line on or even increase acceptable pricing levels. This would include anything that improves product quality or utility to customers. Anything you can economically do to add value or heighten the perception of value offers possibilities for protecting or enhancing gross margin. The same principle holds true for anything you do in terms of direct and indirect customer experiences with your company. These would range from something as fundamental as product design and basic distribution-channel selection to such ancillary factors as packing and shipping. Additional value-creation opportunities abound in most companies. The trick is to motivate and empower people to act on them at their individual levels of influence. Equipping people with cash-driver language is an important early step in that direction.

Distribution Channels & Gross Margin

A major issue in gross-margin analysis is distribution-channel strategy. It is particularly critical for Sally Fegley and her husband, Tom, who built Tom and Sally's Handmade Chocolates Inc., in Brattleboro, Vt., from under $100,000 to over a million dollars in just nine years, and ship to all 50 states and six European countries. But because their 100-year-old handcraft techniques for making chocolate are very labor-intensive, opportunities are fairly limited for economies of scale on the production side as a way of growing their business.

On the selling side, Tom and Sally are evaluating a shift toward direct retailing as a significant growth source. Properly managed, this strategy holds the potential for enormous improvement in gross margins. It is also, however, a major strategic shift that will materially change the character of the business. The change will appreciably affect both their occupancy and labor costs, which will undoubtedly rise significantly with a move into retail. But perhaps the biggest cost will be the management time and energy involved in such a dramatic shift in distribution channels. Consider the business issues involved.

Price, gross margin and distribution-channel strategy are a cluster of issues that need to be evaluated interdependently. The essential questions revolve around identifying the sequence of functions that need to be performed to get the end customer satisfied, and determining for each step in the sequence who can offer the best price and performance. The questions are deceptively simple and don't lend themselves to generalizations.

One broad trend, however, is toward shorter channels with a particular emphasis on direct selling. The demand side of this trend is driven by customers who want to benefit from the lower prices that are often made possible by reducing the number of steps and players in the distribution channel. The supply side was driven initially by larger firms in the early '80s; they began hard-wiring themselves into a network of buyers and sellers operating over dedicated lines and using electronic data interchange (EDI) protocols.

More recently, the Internet has further accelerated the trends toward shorter channels and direct selling to near warp speed, as EDI has now developed Internet capabilities. Internet sales in 1998 totaled about $25 billion, and two-thirds of that was business to business. On the other hand, there is a huge target pool of business-to-business goods currently moving through wholesalers at the rate of $2.5 trillion annually, with gross margins averaging somewhere in the 30% range. Think about that: Thirty percent of $2.5 trillion presents a $750 billion target for gross-margin reclamation from wholesalers. Many producers and dot-coms will be lining up to take aim at a target of that magnitude. And Internet sales growth is catching up to the traditional bricks-and-mortar retail segment of the economy. The direct-selling trend is not limited to the internet; consumer catalog and telephone sales continue to grow. Direct selling is also expanding to business-to-business sales in industries that previously followed less-direct channels.

The Internet has further accelerated the trends toward shorter channels and direct selling to near warp speed.

Dell Computer has prospered largely by taking a leading role in radical channel and supply-chain changes. Jim Schneider, the senior financial vice-president at Dell, emphasizes that channel-analysis questions must focus on the cost-effectiveness with which an enterprise can assume the middleman's value added. Among the first considerations for analyzing the business case will be the effects on: sales-growth rate, the fundamentals, swing factors and capital expenditures. Sound familiar? Channel realignment can easily have an impact on a business at the level of every one of the seven cash drivers.

Probably the major fear and trade-off area in distribution-channel analysis has to be the potential cost of channel clash, as when some middleman starts seeing you as a competitor. For example, an art-supply wholesaler I know began a direct-mail and Internet promotion to end users. This badly damaged relations with many of her longtime retail-store accounts. Bear in mind that if you start selling directly to end-use customers, your former retail accounts may decide to become your competitors by aligning with other producers to replace the volume they lost from you. The biggest risk in that situation may be that those retailers have better relationships with end-use customers than you do and a more in-depth understanding of their needs.

Gross Margin & Totally Perishable 'Inventory'

In service businesses, while there is no inventory in the traditional sense, there is often some resource that you cannot easily just stop and start buying as the marketplace changes. Examples would include airline seats, motel rooms and a staff of professional consultants for hire. In these cases, resource management and supporting information systems become even more critical for maintaining margins because you essentially have to pay for the resource that you *don't* use. You can never again use last night's unoccupied motel room. Unbilled staff hours never come around again. In other words, the service is totally perishable.

Judy Nagengast at Continental Design understands this perishability principle. She and her husband run an organization of more than 320 employees, most of whom work on fairly long-term project assignments in the automotive design and engineering field. The combination of competition and the power of large customers to set prices means that margin improvements can't come on the price side. Maintaining margins in the contract-staffing business depends on keeping professional employees as close to fully billed as possible. Judy keeps this on track with the right balance and teamwork between Continental's recruiting staff and its sales staff. They work hard to keep their information channels clear, accurate and up-to-date. Good sales forecasting integrates almost seamlessly with targeted recruiting. The goal, of course, is never to have to tell a client you don't have the right specialist when needed, but to fulfill client needs without having any more unbilled hours than absolutely required for basics such as training and some minimal administrative demands on the professional's time.

In most respects, this focus on full utilization of fixed or semi-fixed resources is as much an operating-expense issue as it is a gross-margin issue. Let's turn now explicitly to operating expense—that is, selling, general and administrative (SG&A) costs—as a cash driver unto itself.

SG&A: The Other Fundamental

Y OU HAVE BEATEN THE BUSHES TO RAISE THE SALES-growth rate. You have managed to cut the costs of meeting your customer's needs to the lowest level consistent with quality and competitive pressures. You have revised your distribution-channel strategy to broaden your market without sacrificing gross margin. Now you need to focus on operating expense.

Selling, general and administrative expense (SG&A) is usu-ally the next-biggest cash driver after sales growth and gross margins. In a service business especially, this is where most of your costs are unless you explicitly calculate and report a direct cost-of-sales component. In a manufacturing or merchandising business, more of your costs are typically in cost of goods sold, but SG&A is still very significant and includes all the corporate overhead items: the people and functions, the spaces, and resources not directly attributable to the actual product. All normal operating expenses, other than those associated with a physical product (or service offering), are generally found here—salaries, wages, commissions, bonuses, benefit expenses, power, heat, light, rent, leases, operational taxes, travel, enter-tainment, insurance and supplies.

SG&A excludes expenses not associated with the operating elements of the business, such as investment, financing and taxes. Although these categories are important and sometimes significant in size, they are not items you deal with day to day to get your product or service out to the customer.

Cost Ups & Downs

The SG&A category is so inclusive that it is somewhat difficult to generalize about it as a category. But one generalization that can be made is that it is always easier to let expenses go up than it is to bring them back down. This is true whether SG&A is considered in dollars or percentages. The better the organization is doing, the easier it is for costs to creep up. The worse it is doing, the more likely it becomes that when costs *are* finally cut, the cuts will be made quickly and will not be particularly well thought out. If you're bleeding profusely, the efficiency of the bandage isn't closely scrutinized.

The easiest cuts are usually the ones that have the least-immediate impact on the success of the firm. Unfortunately, they are often the cuts that will do the most long-term damage. Consider training, for example, or advertising. There is usually little immediate negative impact on the business when you cut such costs. But if they were good training programs and sensible advertising campaigns, you will reap the bitter fruit of such cuts months or years down the line. Because most businesses normally go through up and down cycles to some degree, it is almost inevitable that you will add fat to the company in the good times and cut at least some muscle in the bad times.

How have you responded to this yo-yo phenomenon in your business? Is there any way to prepare for it or to offset some of its effects? Maybe you could start with being sure you have a clear awareness of how your sphere of influence adds most directly to the organization's success. What are the most important things you do, the next most important, and so forth? Identify the resources you need most critically to effectively and efficiently make your contribution. Preparing in this way will help you develop a much clearer distinction between what is fat and what is muscle. With that distinction more clearly in mind, you can focus on turning fat to muscle during the good times. More muscle to begin with reduces both the likelihood and severity of the eventual bad times. Don't let costs creep up in your area unless they are adding materially to quality, capacity, insight or responsiveness. If you keep the organization aware and informed of where the muscle is, then you and your mission-critical resources will have the best win-win chance of surviving the inevitable cuts when tough times arrive.

SG&A & Capacity

There is an important dimension to SG&A that has to do with capacity. Consider this issue by reflecting on the following questions from the viewpoint of your responsibilities:

What is the relationship generally between resources and revenue growth in your situation?

What resources would have to be added in your area to accommodate a 10% increase in sales? How about a 25% increase?

What resources would such a sales increase affect most severely? You need to know what the biggest constraints are. Maybe it is space, or staff, or computer capacity. Perhaps insufficient parking or the unavailability of some specialized back-ordered resource would leave you short.

What could you least painfully give up if sales volume dropped and you absolutely had to cut costs by 5%? What about a 15% cost reduction?

As you make the mental trade-offs between these two directions, growth and shrinkage, what is your sense of their relative likelihood and probable causes?

What step functions are at play—that is, what capacity-enhancing resources can be bought only in fairly large chunks?

As an example of how that last question might apply to your business, you might have to lease the whole upstairs floor in the building you're in to get more space for just a couple of new hires. Planning ahead for such eventualities almost always creates more options than waiting until the last minute. If, for example, your offices were 85% occupied coming out of the last recession, maybe that was the time to have committed to leasing the whole next floor and subletting to smaller individual users on staggered, short-term leases while you readied your business for the next growth period.

Economies of scale are often an issue with SG&A. It is frequently possible to pay only a small amount more for a lot of additional capacity. Resources as diverse as delivery trucks, advertising space, telephone and computer systems fall into this category. Do your homework. Get a sense of how close to capacity your various resources are. Analyze the upgrade options and the price/performance trade-offs for additional capacity. Then either make the considered decision or pass along the information to the responsible party. Always consider the economy version on elements of both equipment and services. The economy route is not always the best choice, but it helps define the range. For example, unless your computer needs demand state-of-the-art equipment, a system just a year or two old may be sufficient for your needs and cost a fraction of a new model. Various professional services such as attorneys and publicists have widely different rates and retainer levels. If your needs in these areas are relatively simple and straightforward, why pay top dollar for the high-rent professionals when a journeyman practitioner will do as well?

Expense & Expenditure

Thus far, we have been talking primarily about expense-related decisions. The significant cash dimensions of these are obvious. Sometimes, though, what is not nearly so obvious is the distinction between expense and *expenditure*. In your personal life, you usually experience expense and expenditure simultaneously when you buy something. In business, however, there is almost always a time gap between when an expense is incurred and when you actually lay out the cash—that is, make the expenditure.

This difference is at the heart of the cash-versus-accrual differential. Other things being equal, the more you can manage that time gap in your favor, the better your cash flow will be. When I say other things being equal, I want to stress the point that extending the time gap for payment is good so long as it doesn't create other, larger problems. Let's use a simple example. There might be major morale problems if payroll were to be converted from every two weeks to a monthly basis. Sure, it would free up cash; the cash-flow benefit would equal, on average, a bit more than another full week of payroll. But the impact on employee relations would probably not be worth it.

In your personal life, you usually experience expense and expenditure simultaneously when you buy something. In business, however, there is almost always a time gap between when an expense is incurred and when you actually lay out the cash—that is, make the expenditure.

Regarding the sales force, perhaps it could reasonably be argued that the commission portion of earnings shouldn't be paid until the customer invoice is collected. There might be an even stronger case for such a plan if the sales force normally has a direct role in accounts receivable. But even in this common instance, don't make such decisions hastily. Check industry practice. See if there is research or information of any sort on the topic.

In considering delaying commission payments, you may find that some of the connection between sales-force accomplishment and its associated reward is broken. As a result, field sales people could actually wind up performing at a lower level when commission payments are delayed until payment of the associated customer invoice. If this sales underperformance turns out to more than offset the cash-flow value of delay, it is probably best not to stir up that particular hornet's nest. On the other hand, if the selling environment is more relational than merely transactional in nature, it is probably reasonable to operate with your sales force on the basis that no sale is complete until the cash is in the till.

Many companies thread this particular needle by paying sales commissions upon billing but with the understanding that they can be charged back. Chargebacks are most commonly used if the customer invoice remains unpaid for more than some defined period, say 90 days.

After revenue, SG&A is the largest single number on the income statement for service businesses that don't break out cost of sales (or services). For companies that do break out cost of sales (manufacturers, retailers, wholesalers and some service companies) SG&A is typically the second-biggest number, following sales. In the majority of all cases, it is the most controllable or discretionary cost category and therefore warrants careful consideration by senior management with regard to long-term business strategy. Well-managed SG&A is truly fundamental, not just incidental, in almost every business.

As we leave the business fundamentals of gross margins and SG&A, we move on to the swing factors—accounts receivable, inventory and accounts payable. Though less central to the business than the fundamentals, swing factors can sink your business, despite good fundamentals, if they are not carefully controlled. Similarly, they can save your skin if they are managed particularly well when the fundamentals may be temporarily going against you.

Swing Factor #1: Accounts Receivable

T THIS POINT IN THE SEQUENCE OF THE CASH-driver discussion, we have examined sales growth, documented its cost through cost of goods sold, and been left with some gross margin from which to pay SG&A expense. Not much of anything can get paid for, however, until you get paid by your customer. This is precisely why accounts receivable (A/R) is the first and most significant of the class of cash drivers known as swing factors.

By offering customers payment terms other than cash on the barrelhead, you automatically make four assumptions: that the customer has both 1) the *willingness* and 2) the *ability* to pay you; and that neither that 3) ability nor 4) willingness will fail between the time the order is shipped and the time payment is due. But any of those assumptions may turn out to be inaccurate. The better you manage your receivables—the money that is owed for work completed or products delivered—the less likely you are to be bitten by a bad assumption. If you do get bitten from time to time, the cost can be minimized if you have clear policies about how deeply you will allow any account to become indebted, and what steps you will take once further credit is cut off.

Accounts receivable is discussed and measured in *days receivable*, and the calculation is based on in sales dollars. That is to say, divide the dollars of accounts receivable by the dollars of annual sales, and multiply the result by 365 (days per year). (For contractors, costs and profits in excess of billings should be considered a receivable for this purpose. By the same logic, on the liability side, billings in excess of costs—so called front-end loading—could be treated as payables.) If, for example, A/R is $1 million and annual sales is $8 million, then 1/8 x 365 produces an A/R cash-driver value of 45.6. This means that there are that many days worth of sales tied up, or invested, in accounts receivable. Put another way, it takes an average of 45.6 days to collect on the typical sale.

If A/R days move upward from one period to the next, you generally know that some kind of management decision or practice has changed with respect to accounts receivable. If you look only at dollars of A/R from period to period, you learn nothing about the management of receivables per se. That's because the effect of sales growth is factored in when you examine dollar totals. But by checking the relative measure—that is, the cash-driver measure of A/R days—you avoid being distracted by the effect on receivables of changes due to sales level. By looking only at the *relative* measure, A/R days, you narrow the focus to things essentially attributable to A/R management issues. Let's consider the nature of some of those issues.

Communicating With Customers

Accounts-receivable aging reports have been around forever. The reports sort and divide accounts or invoices into 30-, 60- and 90-day categories. Companies used to run these reports no more than monthly. That meant that only customers who were a month or more behind in paying were contacted, which was not terribly efficient. Now, many companies call every new customer on the day after the first invoice-due date, whether or not payment has been received. If the payment has been received, the call is mainly to say thanks. If it has not been received, the call, while reminding the customer that payment is due, offers an opportunity to ask if everything was OK with the order. This approach gently clues new customers into the company's focus on on-time collections at the beginning of the relationship. This initial phone call is also a great time to confirm that the invoice went to the right person at the right address. If it didn't, the invoice can bounce around for quite a while before winding up in the right place, especially in a large company.

Today, with the availability of inexpensive computers and off-the-shelf software, you can generate a receivables aging-report daily, as needed—or better yet, automatically when predetermined triggers are set off.

Human nature being what it is, invoices that are confusing, incomplete, inadequately detailed, hard to read, not well tied to appropriate documentation, hard to follow up on, or otherwise deficient create a significant rise in the probability of delayed payment. Your invoice needs to be as carefully designed and thought through as your marketing pieces and signage. Indeed, it is part of that continuum—in some ways the most important part. Full-disclosure invoices should also clearly set forth payment-date expectations, late-charge policy and information regarding the process for resolving disputes. Marketing's job is to make it easy to buy from you. Accounts receivable's job is to make it easy for customers to pay you.

Your invoice needs to be as carefully designed and thought through as your marketing pieces and signage. Indeed, it is part of that continuum— in some ways the most important part.

Despite best practice in receivables management, sometimes the small firm dealing with large customers is at a disadvantage. As Sally and Tom Fegley, for instance, consider shifting their homemade-chocolates business into selling through their own retail outlets, they hope not only to improve gross margins but also to solve some accounts-receivable problems. The biggest such problem is that many very large specialty retailers have taken advantage of them at two levels: payment terms, and return or charge-back policies. More growth through their own retail outlets would help minimize the effects of these often hidden costs. At the other end of the size spectrum, the Fegleys have had to deal with the risk associated with shipping to small retail outlets. With many of these accounts, Tom and Sally ship only on firm credit card orders. And as a general rule they never ship first orders on credit except to large, reputable companies. This can be a good first-pass way to weed out many con artists.

A/R & the Marketing Connection

In managing accounts receivable, don't let marketing and accounting work at cross-purposes. Your A/R staff needs to be sensitive to the probability that delinquent customers are valued clients who are just temporarily behind. Similarly, your marketing and sales people need to have some sense of urgency about getting—and keeping—their customers current on payment obligations. Potential conflict can be reduced with good interdepartmental communications, which could include getting the departments together to jointly solve problems. At Office Plan Inc., the office furniture re-furbisher we looked at in an earlier chapter, receivables management is helped greatly by requiring 50% down payments at the time of contract for most sales. Another less tangible, yet very real, help is that the sales people are also stockholders; their equity participation in the company. Not too surprisingly, Office Plan has no bad debt!

Sometimes tailored payment terms for a certain customer, or easier payment terms across the board can be an important part of the marketing mix. You might want to utilize such terms to react to competitive pressures, to introduce a new product, to respond to the seasonal needs of a customer, or for a variety of sales and marketing tactics. Before you change payment terms, make sure you have the full support of your accounts receivable, accounting and finance staff. Part of that support is helping to analyze the true costs and cash-flow implications of the strategy. This helps ensure that genuinely sound trade-offs can be made in the best interests of the firm as a whole rather than reflecting the more parochial interests of a particular department.

Important marketing issues that have potentially significant impact on cash-flow arise whenever we consider distribution-channel strategy or development of export sales. Amgen Inc. is a case in point. This pharmaceutical firm has the best record in its industry for management of receivables, inventory and payables. On the A/R side, the reasons are clearly trace-able to two key differences between Amgen and most of the rest of its indus-try. First, Amgen relies more on whole-salers than do its competitors, who sell more directly to retailers. The difference in A/R terms is significant because whole-sale trade terms bring cash in more than twice as fast as retail terms. Second, Amgen's sales are far more skewed to the domestic market than are its more inter-nationally minded competitors. The dif-ference is important because in most for-eign markets, collection cycles are longer than in the U.S. It would be interesting to see how well Amgen would fare if cash-flow management comparisons with its industry were to be adjusted for these natural advantages. Even more to the point is the impact these issues might have if and when Amgen shifts to a more direct-channel strategy or seeks growth in export markets.

> **In managing accounts receivable, don't let marketing and accounting work at cross-purposes. Your A/R staff needs to be sensitive to the probability that delinquent customers are valued clients, and your marketing and sales people need to have some sense of urgency about getting —and keeping—their customers current on payment obligations.**

Industry Norms

Often, payment terms are so well established in an industry that not much can be done directly to increase the speed of collections. But indirect mea-sures can often be helpful. For example, if you have excess or inexpensive inventory storage available, you might take on some of the client's warehousing function but still get paid as though the full order had been delivered. Here, the trade-offs are issues of timing, delivery and economical shipping quanti-ty. Another indirect approach to A/R management may involve advance deposits or other forms of prepayment on special orders. These reduce the A/R balance by never even allowing it in the first place.

In the construction, defense and aerospace industries especially, there are opportunities for early payment because of the longer term and custom nature of the individual jobs. In reality, these situations don't so much represent early payment as they do a different concept of what constitutes a billable event. To the extent that you can redefine your own billable events to accelerate them, you will improve cash flow. A related idea in a service business is to develop retainer-basis billing instead of purely project-based, event-oriented billing. You may not get paid any sooner on average, but you will enjoy a more predictable cash flow.

To the extent that a new customer's financial statements are available or could be made available, why not apply cash-flow thinking to that client's financials as part of the credit-review process? After all, it is only cash that can ultimately pay for the product you ship or the service you render.

When there are industry disturbances such as strikes, demand spikes, or shortages of product, you might be able to shorten payment terms. When the disturbance passes, you might be able to continue the shorter term. Also keep a close watch on the validity of payment discounts that customers take based on your published terms. Be vigilant especially with new customers, to educate them as to your expectations so that they don't take a 2% discount for payment within ten days as permitted by your invoice when in fact they are actually paying in 20 or 30 days.

Most medium size and larger businesses that sell to other businesses have a credit-check function. The task is to investigate and evaluate prospective new customers' creditworthiness. There are a wide variety of sources and methods to help with this process, including setting limits on A/R balances. One element that is often overlooked is the subject of this book—cash flow. To the extent that a new customer's financial statements are available or could be made available, why not apply cash-flow thinking to that client's financials as part of the review process? After all, it is only cash that can ultimately pay for the product you ship or the service you render. If the new customer is in cash-flow trouble, chances are that your receivables from that customer will be in trouble before very long, too.

If the size and value of a particular customer make it worthwhile, do the work necessary to analyze its financial need. If you know more about its cash-flow situation, you might craft terms more creatively without adding undue risk. If your company sells large-ticket items to other businesses, it also helps to have an established policy about when your senior management gets involved in the collection effort. CEO Judy Nagengast at Continental Design always makes personal client contact if an account hits 90 days. Most of the time, the personal impact of CEO contact both accelerates payment and educates the customer that timely payment is a high priority. Other techniques include top-ten lists as to both dollar and time delinquency, as well as specific dollar thresholds that prompt earlier senior-management involvement.

Factoring

When your business receivables are of good quality, they are readily marketable to specialist financiers called factors. A factor buys your receivables at a discount, advancing cash as you make shipments, thereby freeing up most of your investment in A/R for more productive uses. The factor also assumes most of your credit-related functions and can do so on a non-notification basis—that is, your customers are not aware that their receivable has been sold to the factor. Factoring is an attractive option if you need cash, but it is also somewhat expensive compared with other cash-generating alternatives. Because of the expense, which runs from about 3% to 10% of the A/R's face value, it may be suitable for your company only if one or more of the following circumstances apply:

■ **you have no other choice due to lack of credit,** for whatever reasons;

■ **you can readily justify the cost by margins** to be made on sales that would otherwise be forgone; or

■ **you are in a business with severe seasonal fluctuations** that make year-round A/R departments hard to justify.

There are two main reasons that factoring is often over-looked as a financing choice—cost and lack of knowledge. Factoring is considered a last recourse because of its high cost. On the other hand, the cost-savings potential associated with factoring effectively includes the outsourcing of most A/R functions as an integral part of the service. For example, if you sell your receivables, you might need fewer people in your accounting department. In addition to the savings in salary and benefits, the space that the A/R staff formerly occupied can be used by employees who are more directly involved in producing revenue. Or you might be able to delay running out of space and having to move to larger quarters.

Many people still think of factoring as a specialized tool for just the garment and related industries, where it got its start. But any firm with good-quality receivables from businesses or government entities can qualify for a factoring relationship.

One reason factoring is considered high-cost is that the wrong basis for cost comparison is often used. If A/R turns 12 times a year and your average net cost paid to the factor is 6% on each invoice, then the resulting 72% seems high compared with borrowing from the bank at 10%. The cost may still seem high after counting what you save, directly and indirectly by not having to maintain your own A/R staff. But since you are by definition strapped for cash to begin with, how would you pay the bank back? And if there is no adequate payback plan, what bank would lend you money in the first place? So, the bank at 10% versus the factor at 72% is really not the appropriate comparison if bank financing is not available. The real comparison should be with the additional dollars of contribution margin you earn on the incremental sales that you can ship because you *don't* have to carry all the A/R balances. A final note on cost comparisons: For a great many enterprises that do use factors, the only real alternative for raising additional capital is selling equity, and even in cases where that choice is feasible, it is likely to be still more expensive.

The second major reason factoring is often overlooked as a financing option is simply a knowledge gap. Many people still think of factoring as a specialized tool for just the garment and related industries, where it got its start. But any firm with good-quality receivables from businesses or government entities can qualify for a factoring relationship. You should consider that option whenever conventional lower-cost methods are not available, or when the administrative A/R functions the factor can perform are a priority for you. Most often, as mentioned earlier, a high degree of seasonality in your order flow may make maintaining an adequate A/R function of your own too expensive on a year-round basis.

One way or another, whether on your own or through a factor, no sooner do you get on top of A/R management than you realize that you have almost as much money tied up in inventory as you did in A/R. Thus, we look next at swing factor number two—inventory.

Swing Factor #2: Inventory

HAVING DEALT SUCCESSFULLY WITH MANAGEMENT OF your accounts receivable (A/R), you are now ready to ship another truckload of the fine products sitting in your inventory to good customers who will pay on time. As with A/R, inventory is also measured and calculated in days. Unlike A/R, which is based on sales dollars, inventory is denominated in cost-of-goods-sold dollars. The reason is simple. A/R represents sales that have already been made and so is related to sales. But what remains in inventory is, by definition, not yet sold, so it is both valued at cost and related to cost.

Inventory days is the average number of days of production value and purchases sitting in inventory at the end of the period. It is calculated by dividing end-of-year inventory dollars by the year's cost-of-goods-sold dollars, then multiplying by 365 days. It may be helpful to think of inventory days as the average number of days an item waits in inventory before it is sold and thereby converted from inventory to accounts receivable. Inventory days tends to rise somewhat with the number of steps in the distribution channel. This is a natural consequence of the statistical inefficiencies required to maintain buffer stocks at more points along the distribution chain.

Another dimension of inventory days that needs to be considered is where the company is in its business year when its accounting year ends. On a natural fiscal-year basis geared to the firm's natural seasonal pattern, the end of the accounting year will generally coincide with an inventory low point, and so a year-end inventory-days calculation would be misleading if understood as being normal through the rest of the year.

Thus, the more seasonal any business is, the more important it becomes to forecast, track and manage cash flow on shorter intervals. A good weekly cash-flow projection, for example, helps New Covenant Care, a multistate operator of nursing homes and assisted-living centers, to schedule routine capital expenditures. Although this is not a seasonal business in the traditional sense, because the majority of New Covenant's revenue comes from government entities and is paid on the basis of preset cycles for actual days of care, revenue can be forecasted quite precisely. As a consequence, the company is able to schedule furniture and carpeting replacements a year in advance to match the cash-flow peaks.

> **The most commonly used method in American business for valuing inventory is LIFO (last in, first out)—that is, the last item into your inventory is the first one out for costing purposes.**

Inventory Valuation

The method used to value your inventory for balance-sheet purposes is an important issue in inventory management. When a sale is made from an inventory of many identical units that may have been acquired or manufactured over a considerable time period at different cost levels, the question arises as to what cost to charge to cost of sales. Is it the average cost, the oldest cost, the most recent cost? Each method has its pros and cons, but the most commonly used method in American business is LIFO (last in, first out)—that is, the last item into your inventory is the first one out for costing purposes. Another way to say it is that you use your most recent cost data for charging inventory to cost of sales.

In the absence of significant inflation or general price-rise trends in your industry, the valuation method you use doesn't make much difference. But in a time of generally rising prices, using LIFO will match your highest, most recent cost against sales for calculation of profit. Highest cost obviously means lowest profit, and so LIFO inventory valuation will tend to understate profits in times of rising prices. Over an extended period, that understatement can add up to a significant sum because you may be selling older inventory that cost you less to purchase. In addition to understating profit a bit, LIFO will also tend to understate the implied cost of replacing your inventory. That's because whatever remains in inventory is carried at the oldest, and presumably lowest, cost level. This LIFO issue may seem to be one of those arcane accounting issues that cause most nonaccountants' eyes to glass over, but you should be aware of it because of the cash-flow impact. To the extent that LIFO understates profit, you thereby improve cash flow by an amount equal to the out-of-pocket taxes you saved on the profit understatement.

In a time of rising prices, using LIFO will match your highest, most recent cost against sales for calculation of profit. Highest cost obviously means lowest profit, and so LIFO inventory valuation will tend to understate profits in these times. Over an extended period, that understatement can add up to a significant sum because you may be selling older inventory that cost you less to purchase.

For many businesses, inventory valuation is relatively straightforward because both inventory and sales remain fairly constant over the course of the year. In some more highly seasonal businesses, however, inventory can take huge swings. Take the pickle industry, for example. At the height of the season, packers buy every cucumber available from contracted growers in several surrounding states. Jars, lids and labels arrive daily at the plant to accommodate the season's peak. Hundreds of short-term and part-time workers overflow the parking lots as companies scramble to produce a year's worth of inventory in just a few months. Then for the rest of the year, the inventory is sold down. But here the reduction of inventory is not as gradual and smooth as one might expect because demand also has a strong seasonal nature.

Like the management of a pickle-packing firm, your management must understand your business's unique patterns. It is also important to be sure your banker understands such uniqueness because the cash-flow implications are so significant. Banks tend to specialize broadly in their lending organization, especially in specialized areas. So if you were in the agriculture-related pickle business, it is fairly likely that your lender would have a good feel for seasonal patterns because of the inherently seasonal nature of agriculture. Other industries' seasonal needs may be less obvious and require you to educate your banker.

> **There are three types of inventory: raw materials, work in process and finished goods. In a merchandising business, goods available for sale are all there is. Manufacturers and contractors of various types deal with all three types of inventory.**

In still other businesses, events can create uneven inventory patterns that recur but are not based on predictable patterns. Susan McCloskey of the furniture refurbishing company Office Plan works hard to make sure her bank understands her business. Buying out a few floors of used office furniture several times a year creates large swings in inventory investment. Because of those swings, her usage of the bank line of credit bounces around quite a bit. Keeping the bank informed helps, and one of the more important tools in keeping the bankers informed is Susan's weekly cash-flow report.

Types of Inventory

There are three types of inventory: raw materials, work in process and finished goods. In a merchandising business, goods available for sale are all there is. Manufacturers and contractors of various types deal with all three types of inventory. Of course, one firm's finished-goods inventory can be another's raw material. Intel's computer chips are a finished product for Intel but a raw material to Dell. When the chip is mounted on a motherboard as the computer is assembled, the chip becomes work in process, along with the direct labor and all associated factory overhead as allocated to complete the mounting step. As other parts are added and tested step by step, the value of work in process grows for that unit. When the last elements of labor, factory overhead and material are added, the computer is finally moved from work in process into finished-goods inventory and considered ready for sale.

As parts and pieces are added along the production line, many businesses consider whether the number of parts or steps can be reduced as a way reducing production and inventory costs. A related consideration is often missed, however. That is whether the number of *different* parts can be reduced. Sometimes a product uses several sizes of screws and tubing, for example, when standardization could create considerable savings. This can easily be the case even if it results in some degree of excess strength or capacity.

Product design and production design can often contribute to improved cash flow by improving the timing of the various steps as an item moves from raw material to finished goods.

Honda has taken advantage of standardization by creating a basic product platform for its Accord frame worldwide. But you don't have to be a global giant to take advantage of the principle. And if you do sell multinationally and produce different versions for each market, consider standardizing by redesigning your product to permit local-market customization. This can significantly reduce inventory while simplifying its management. Hewlett-Packard did this by shipping a standard base-unit printer to a few overseas warehouses, which then did the individual country customization as demand required.

Product design and production design can often contribute to improved cash flow by improving the timing of the various steps as an item moves from raw material to finished goods. How much of the total cost is added at various phases of production is an element of financial engineering that often gets ignored except in some of the largest companies. The financial-engineering dimension needs to be considered along with more conventional product or production engineering. Let's consider an example.

Inventory & the Production Process

The Williams Oilfield Contracting Co.'s manufacturing process called for adding a major, expensive subassembly near the start of a long production process. The only reason the subassembly was being installed at that point was because it was sealed inside the larger assembly by welding. Because of the heat sensitivity of other subsequently installed components, the welding had to be done very early. But did the subassembly have to be installed so early in the process, thus tying up more dollars in inventory than necessary?

It turned out that the subassembly could be obtained from the supplier quickly, as needed, and didn't require much additional labor to integrate into the product late in the process. In fact, the subassembly was not really needed until after a firm customer order was received. A partial redesign replaced welding by bolting together two halves. The expensive subassembly could now be added at the end of the manufacturing process. The result was that 20% of the total cost of finished goods was now added on the day of shipment rather than on day four of a 40-day production cycle. The result was an 18% reduction in inventory days!

But the savings didn't end there. A smart transportation division manager noticed the company could have the supplier ship the expensive subassembly directly to the customer's site and have field installation people add it as part of the site set-up and checkout process. That would save the double shipping expense and pick up another few days of cash flow on investment in the subassembly. In turn, the invoicing section manager in accounting realized that because the invoice traveled with the product and the company was shipping sooner without any change in terms or invoicing practice, a fraction more was cut off of the company's A/R cash-driver days.

This example illustrates how cash-flow thinking in several departments can make a business run better. Like other aspects of a business, inventory management can be regarded from different perspectives. From a narrow sales and marketing point of view, every item, in every size and color, with an infinite variety of features, should always be available to ship today for overnight delivery to any customer anywhere, and carry a ten-year warranty. From an equally narrow production point of view, there should be only one size and one color, the basic feature mix should be standardized, and there should be one long, continuous production run. Meanwhile, the head of the finance department will want to minimize investment in inventory, which means very short production runs, and making product only on receipt of firm orders with 50% deposits. And he'd eliminate the warranty and sell long-term service policies instead.

Narrow departmental perspectives are not good for growing, healthy companies. Many times, however, such a narrow focus governs because of strong personalities, lack of analysis or, perhaps most frequently, because the firm has not internalized the cash-flow concept and the cash-driver mindset. Cash-flow issues and cash-driver thinking are part of everybody's responsibility. As they were at the Williams Oilfield Contracting Co., they should be basic tools in the kit of every responsible member of your management team. As you keep looking for ways to make cash flow faster and work more efficiently, you'll find it arrives sooner from others and stays longer in your hands.

Just-in-Time (JIT) Inventory

With proper planning, Rome *could* have been built in a day. Maybe. The point is that with careful planning and design, huge improvements can be made in almost anything. Just-in-time (JIT) inventory management aims to reverse inventory movement from a push to a pull approach as a strategy for radical inventory reduction. Here is a simplified example of JIT in action. At 8:30 one morning, a customer orders an item from a sales rep, who calls the order in immediately. Shipping notifies final assembly to complete one more unit. Final assembly calls the platform, power and accessory departments, each of which in turn notifies a work cell to get ready to start. The cells call vendors whose trucks will be dispatched with the necessary parts and materials just in time to deliver to the work cells by the end of the lunch break. Soon, the three cells will have pooled the talents of their individual members to get the job done and forwarded their finished power, platform and accessory packages to final assembly. Just in time, final assembly does its thing flawlessly and passes the ball to shipping, which runs the invoice, packages the product carefully and gets it on the last truck before the five o'clock whistle. Whew.

For just-in-time inventory management to work, your suppliers and workers alike have to embrace the concept.

For JIT to work, your suppliers and workers alike have to embrace the concept. You'll work with fewer suppliers, who will become strategic partners, delivering all of what you want, exactly when you want it, with absolute assurance of quality. What's more, they will do it in just the quantity needed, in as little as a few hours, if they wish to remain strategic partners.

As for your workers, they'll have to turn from a highly specialized and fragmented assembly-line mentality to the work-cell concept. That requires having multiskilled, cross-trained workers, each of whom does a variety of tasks. One of the most important tasks is communication with other work cells, or *islands*, both upstream and downstream in the production flow.

The payoff for effective JIT inventory systems was originally a very significant, often enormous reduction in inventory investment, along with reduced inventory carrying costs. JIT proponents envisioned the virtual elimination of inventory pools at each level—raw material, work in process, and finished goods. These were seen as stagnant backwaters of inefficiency where cash just sat and didn't flow until someone opened the floodgates in the dam to push some inventory downstream. With JIT production processes, inventory is now *pulled* downstream as demand requires.

Over time, JIT has evolved from its origins as simply an inventory-reduction system and has become more of a total philosophy. The cash-driver philosophy has a clear parallel with JIT. The key in both cases is *flow*. Nothing in the business should be static; all should be in flow. If an element of inventory is static, it is losing value. Every element of inventory should either be in the process of having value added or it should be in motion to the next place where value can be added. The same is true for information, for people, and every other resource.

Everyone and everything in the system should be actively adding value, having value added, or be enroute to a value-adding worksite at all times. It's all about flow, movement, and turnover, in the service of adding value, quality, and efficiency.

Inventory & Purchasing Management

Merchandising presents a somewhat different set of inventory problems from those encountered with manufacturing or contracting. Purchasing management is especially critical in this area and continues to become proportionally more so as questions of obsolescence, trends and fashions come into play. Nothing loses value faster than last season's hot color or the hi-tech toy that has been replaced by the multigigabyte, whiz-bang model. As with every other dimension of the business, the right information at the right time, in the right form, is enormously important. This is probably more generally true with inventory than any other area of the business. The reason is simply because inventory is usually the most perishable asset, the one most subject to rapid decline in value if you misstep just a bit on trend, style, color or rate of technological change. This gets especially tricky when you realize that there is a built-in Catch-22. The hotter a particular product, the more we want to stock up on it to meet what we hope will be some very profitable demand. But one characteristic of what is hot today is that it usually drops off in demand much more quickly than what was never more than lukewarm.

Slow-but-steady sellers are a lot less risky. In inventory terms, they stay on the shelf longer and are rarely as profitable on a per-unit basis as what's hot. The trade-off, however, is that we seldom have to worry about the steady-eddie products having to be disposed of at super-steep markdowns.

Most grocery products lie almost at the extreme low end of the inventory-risk scale, and yet the Hannaford Bros. Co., a major supermarket chain, has invested heavily in inventory-control systems to accurately track what is actually moving out the door. In contrast, most of its competitors *estimate* what is moving out the door by looking at what is moving from the warehouse to the stores, and then doing quick samples of what remains on the shelf to back into sales estimates by product. Hannaford knows *exactly* what is selling, and that information precision has enabled it to materially improve its forecast of demand. This has advanced to a point where Hannaford has been able to decrease inventory holdings in days by 5% while simultaneously reducing the number of out-of-stock conditions that disappoint customers, create ill will and lose margins. Besides these obvious costs associated with out-of-stock conditions, there are also hidden costs. These can take a number of forms, including forgone economies of scale that might have been enjoyed if just-in-time inventory had made it possible to achieve larger quantity discounts, lower per-unit transportation costs and longer production runs.

Inventory-Related Costs

We have just reviewed some of the costs of *not* having enough inventory. Let's now consider the more direct costs associated *with* holding inventory. The largest cost is usually the capital cost on the inventory investment. If you have lots of borrowing room, that cost is often not much more than just the interest cost at your bank. If, though, you have little or no credit left, or are growing at a very high rate, the capital cost of carrying inventory jumps to a much higher level—to the lost-profit level called the *opportunity cost*. That is the alternative return you could get by using funds invested in inventory elsewhere in your business, most typically through selling more high-margin product.

Consider an example: You are fully leveraged and cannot borrow more capital, so the brake on sales growth is the amount of cash available to finance A/R, which you believe is already as tightly managed as you can make it. If you could just free up $25,000 cash by better inventory management, you could sell $50,000 more per month, assuming an average 100% markup. A $25,000 reduction in inventory seems achievable because it is only 10% of your total inventory, net of the related payables. Inventory is turning over an average of 12 times a year (30 days inventory), so at a 35% contribution margin, you may be willing to spend quite a bit to get enough control over inventory to be able to cut it the requisite 10%.

Enter the highly recommended inventory-control specialist with charts, formulas, computers and software. He has just come from doing that bang-up inventory-control system at Hannaford Bros. and thinks your potential to cut inventory investment is at least double Hannaford's in proportional terms because your current system is only minimally automated. He's got an all-inclusive inventory-control package deal, including training your people in its use for a total cost of $25,000 in up-front licensing and consulting fees, and $2,000 per month for a maintenance contract. Is that a deal? Probably, since $50,000 per month extra sales multiplied by 0.35 contribution margin results in $17,500 monthly additional contribution before tax.

If you have little or no credit left, or are growing at a very high rate, the capital cost of carrying inventory jumps to a higher level— to the lost-profit level called the *opportunity cost*. That is the alternative return you could get by using funds invested in inventory elsewhere in your business, most typically through selling more high-margin product.

Before deciding on the consultant's proposal, maybe you need to look at the full array of inventory-related costs. They fall into categories that can be described in a number of ways. Most commonly they are laid out as ordering cost, carrying cost, and the one we looked at a little earlier, the cost of running out of stock. Carrying cost is the largest of the three and has several components, the largest of which is cost of capital. There are, however, a couple of other financial costs as well: taxes and insurance. There are also *physical* carrying costs that include storage and handling. Finally, there are inventory risk costs including deterioration, pilferage and obsolescence. If you have never done so, at least roughly estimate each of these costs for your own firm, and use the resulting total as part of the trade-off analysis that you do in inventory planning. This is especially important for calculating the basic inventory-management measure known as economic order quantity (EOQ). Let's explore that concept a bit more deeply.

Economic Order Quantity (EOQ)

The first thing you will want to do with the estimates you work out for the carrying cost of inventory is to plug them into the formula for calculating economic order quantity. This formula will minimize the sum of carrying costs and ordering costs for you. Recall that *carrying* costs are the financial, the physical and the risk costs as outlined above. *Ordering* costs generally consist simply of clerical and transportation elements. With a minor modification, this same formula can help you determine economic production run length. Let's see some examples from Jones Dynamite Co.'s experience: The annual carrying cost per unit per year for 2,500 units of a particular product is $1.45. Placing the purchase order, transportation charges and invoice processing through accounts payable costs $28. The EOQ formula is:

$$E = \sqrt{\frac{2QP}{C}}$$

E = economic order quantity
Q = number of annual quantity used
C = annual carrying cost per unit
P = cost of placing the purchase order, transportation and processing the invoice through accounts payable).

In Jones's case, the annual quantity of one of its product lines (Q) is 2,500 units; the annual carrying cost per unit (C) is $1.45; and the cost of processing the order (P) is $28. Plugging those numbers into the formula, we get:

$$\sqrt{\frac{2(2,500)(28)}{1.45}} = 311 \text{ as the EOQ.}$$

Let's shift to the version of the formula for a manufacturer, one of Jones's suppliers, that wants to calculate economic production-run length. The formula remains the same, but (P) becomes setup cost rather than ordering cost. The carrying cost (C) is $0.35 unit; annual volume shipped (Q) is 75,000; and setup costs for the production run (P) is $450. Plugging the numbers in, we calculate the economic run length as:

$$\sqrt{\frac{2(75,000)(450)}{0.35}} = 13,887$$

This is the number of units that will minimize the sum of carrying costs and setup costs.

Think for a moment about why you need such a formula. If you place only one order, or do one production setup, you automatically minimize the order or setup costs. As a result, however, the single-order approach means that you *maximize* your carrying cost. This is because of the much greater average number of units in inventory. At the other extreme, you can minimize carrying cost by ordering or producing only to meet actual needs as they arise. This solution, though, would push *setup or order costs* through the roof. The formula solves your dilemma by minimizing *total cost* as longer runs or bigger orders are offset in their associated costs against longer periods of carrying costs. The formula simply calculates the trade-offs between the two types of costs to help find a reasonable range for decision making.

Ultimately, of course, all of your decisions about inventory will have a customer impact. It is that perspective from which we finally have to evaluate what has been decided. We, too, are somebody's customer and buy most of our inventory on credit. Let's look now at the measure of that cash driver as we consider accounts payable.

Swing Factor #3: Accounts Payable

CCOUNTS PAYABLE IS, OF COURSE, THE FLIP SIDE OF accounts receivable (A/R). Accounts payable is also measured in days, but days worth of cost of goods sold, rather than days of sales as with accounts receivable. There's a simple explanation. Accounts payable is more closely related to inventory, which is valued at cost, while accounts receivable is inherently measured in the selling prices by which you record what the customer owes you. What we say about our customers from an accounts-receivable viewpoint is very much like our own position on accounts payable. That is, the money that is a payable on our books is a receivable to someone else, so we can think reciprocally about the two.

Suppliers & Inventory

A ccounts payable are for products or services that have been acquired and flowed into inventory but have not yet been paid for. They represent a net lessening of, or offset to, your investment in inventory. Because of this inventory connection, accounts-payable dollar totals and inventory dollar totals often move together. If inventory is rising considerably faster than accounts payable, then you may be paying too quickly. Another reason for significantly different rates of change between payables and inventory, however, may simply be differences in supplier terms or product mix.

Some suppliers are big enough that their terms are *the* terms. They are the standard, and you have to live with them. In many cases, though, suppliers will negotiate to get and keep your business. And negotiation implies more than just price. If you are getting into a new product category or expanding into a new market area, your business will likely represent net new volume to a supplier. In such cases, there often will be a willingness to stretch terms considerably. If your new direction prospers, then the supplier will prosper with you. If it doesn't go so well, at least the supplier helped a bit by allowing you to delay payment and thereby spread your risk over a longer time horizon. The key is to make such discussions with suppliers part of the original negotiation.

> **Some suppliers are big enough that their terms are *the* terms. They are the standard, and you have to live with them. In many cases, though, suppliers will negotiate to get and keep your business.**

Financial Proformas Inc., of Walnut Creek, Cal., took this approach when it decided to go beyond its live seminar business and extend it into a packaged series of self-study training volumes. These could be sold on either a stand-alone basis or as part of a live-seminar engagement. The start-up costs for the new program were high. Writers, editors, designers and printers were enlisted, and a great deal of their work was negotiated on a delayed-payment basis. This all represented net new sales volume to them, and if the new line was successful, more volume could be expected. Everyone went into the new venture with eyes wide open, and as a result something worthwhile was created without Financial Proformas incurring new debt or sacrificing equity in the conventional sense. The key, of course, was up-front negotiation and a deliberate choice to participate.

This same principle of up-front negotiation with good suppliers applies if your business is seasonal. Although your cash flow may be pretty stable on a year-to-year basis, strong seasonal patterns may put month-to-month or quarter-to-quarter cash flow on a roller coaster. Sales may be seasonal. Production may be seasonal. SG&A may have some seasonality to it. Whatever the cause or dimensions of your seasonality, it will almost always prove helpful to negotiate the timing of expected payment with everyone to whom you are likely to owe money.

Discounts

Supplier discounts for early payment are often the best return on investment available. Let's look at this assertion more closely. If you do not take advantage of discounts for early payment, at least you need to be aware of what you are passing up. But if you have a young firm with a very high growth rate, you may be wise to pass them up. The cash that is freed up by waiting full term to cover payables can be better utilized in accounts receivable where it will support incremental sales on which you earn full margins. The question is, fuller than what? If terms are 2% discount for payment in ten days or full payment in 30 days, the opportunity is 2% on the *difference* of 20 days. Simple arithmetic shows that a 2% return for every twenty days adds up to more than 36% per year. If you are growing rapidly as a new company with limited alternative sources of cash, you might already be earning that same 36% or more as a contribution margin on each and every turn of your accounts receivable five to ten times a year. By contrast, in a more mature firm or one with more access to capital or a significantly lower growth rate, the discount for early payment yielding 36% per year is reasonably attractive.

There is an aspect of discounts and payables that is often overlooked, even by very cash-sensitive companies. That is the discount frequently available by buying certain items from cash-and-carry discounters rather than on account from suppliers who deliver and bill you. Especially in today's environment of superstores, big-box retailers and the Internet, the convenience of delivery and invoicing from traditional suppliers, on whom you need to rely for some things, can be a real extravagance for some purchases.

Prioritizing & Policing Payables

Payables priorities in many companies are set by categories. Typical top-priority payables are fixed expenses such as payroll and occupancy items. Second-priority payables usually consist of regular vendors of critical services. Also in this category are primary suppliers whose flow of material or services is essential to your ability to meet your customers' delivery schedules.

Policing payables is really just basic good sense. It consists of instituting a set of practices to ensure the matching of your documentation through the system. Purchase orders and shipping documents need to be compared with the invoice. Quantities billed need to be double-checked against receipts; and ancillary items such as delivery charges or sales taxes should be reviewed at least periodically.

Policing payables is really just basic good sense. It consists of instituting a set of practices to ensure the matching of your documentation through the system.

Aging is usually associated primarily with accounts receivable, but it is important with accounts payable as well. Sort and list your payables in age groupings of 30, 60 and 90 days. This will give you a simple, but direct, early warning of possible cash-flow problems, as well as a heads-up on possible sources of liens about to be filed.

A concept closely related to accounts payable is accrued expense, which is often associated with costs found under SG&A. This category is for expenses already incurred but not yet paid for. You have gotten the value but have not yet paid the provider of the service. Taxes of various sorts, such as payroll taxes, can be significant here. So, too, can utilities, commissions and a wide range of other costs, including interest. The main point, of course, is that whether we're speaking of payables or accrued expenses, what we have, in effect, is an interest-free loan in those amounts.

The practice in many enterprises is to pay down the payable and accrual amounts quickly when cash flow is strong and then stretch them out when cash gets thin. This may help share the good times with suppliers and also enable you to take advantage of special discounts for prompt payment. A better approach, however, may be to be as consistent as possible with suppliers. That way you will neither confuse them with uneven behavior nor create expectations that may be frustrated later as you encounter changed circumstances.

The discussion about the cash driver known as accounts-receivable days noted the need to educate customers, especially new customers, about your expectations on payment. A similar process often takes place going the other way. Many companies begin to test supplier expectations by paying at the latest possible time within the allowable terms at first, then progressively extending just one more day each month until the supplier's attention is elicited. In practical terms this may be as simple a process as keeping the checks in the desk drawer one extra day before mailing them to suppliers. The next month it is two days in the drawer, and so forth, until the limits of acceptability for each supplier are reasonably well defined. There is, however, an ethical problem here as well as the practical one of keeping track of how long you can delay each supplier. The ethical problem, of course, is that the transaction was entered into based on an agreement on terms; business needs to honor that trust function, not abuse it. And if you take as much rope as the supplier permits, there may well be no slack left for those times when you might really need to extend payment.

If you take as much rope as the supplier permits, there may well be no slack left for those times when you might really need to extend payment.

In fact, for each cash driver, there is the question of leaving a little slack in the system. If every item is always pushed to the limit, then the tension of the system can make it difficult to absorb the ordinary shocks that circumstances inevitably deal to a business. So, for example, if all of your swing factors are always tuned to their highest state of efficiency, and if that state becomes your normal one, then what room for adjustment is left for responding to cash-flow crises as they come along? A final note on the swing factors, therefore, is to remember that if the fundamentals (gross margins and SG&A) of the business are deteriorating, the swing factors can usually be tightened up a bit to create some cash breathing space while you try to get the fundamentals back on track. The fundamentals, though, *are* fundamental and you will have only a very finite opportunity to correct them.

We have now covered issues of sales growth, the fundamentals and the swing factors. It is time to turn to capital expenditures (Capex) where we do so much of our resource planning for the future.

Keeping Up: Capital Expenditures

HE THINGS THAT COME MOST READILY TO MIND when we think about capital expenditures (Capex) are land, buildings, machinery and equipment. Offices, stores, warehouses and factories are clearly major elements. Production, shipping, computing and other hardware items are still another. With the exception of land, all of these are depreciable assets; you don't account for their cost as an expense when you acquire them, but rather you depreciate them over their useful life, taking a fraction of the original expenditure as an expense to be allocated in each accounting period.

Publicly traded companies produce cash-flow statements that show depreciation and capital expenditures, but many small and medium-size companies do not. (By the time you've reached this part of the book, though, I hope you are convinced your company should be using this statement.) In the absence of a cash-flow statement, you'll have to determine actual capital expenditures on your own by referring to the balance sheets and income statement. The procedure, fortunately, is quite simple.

To calculate net capital expenditures, take the sum of depreciation and amortization expenses from the income statement, and add any increase in net fixed assets between the starting and ending balance sheets. If the net fixed assets declined over the period, subtract the amount of the decline from total depreciation and amortization. Arithmetically, therefore, if net fixed assets declined by an amount equal to total depreciation and amortization, then there were zero net capital expenditures during that period—not at all an uncommon situation.

Depreciable Life & Economic Shifts

Depending on your business and the asset under consideration, normal depreciation schedules may not adequately represent the true cost associated with that item's contribution to revenue during the period. For example, a piece of production equipment may have an economically useful life well beyond its depreciable life. In such a case, profits are understated in the earlier years and overstated in the later years. The reverse is true when an asset has a longer depreciable than economic life. Often this is because the item becomes economically and technologically obsolete before it becomes functionally obsolete. Computers are a good example. Most older computers still work fine for what they were originally acquired to do. The problem is that you may want them to perform functions they weren't designed to do, or they perform in such cumbersome and time-consuming ways that you have judged them unacceptable and obsolete, though they are only a few years old.

As computer technology continues its trend of rapid price-performance improvement, it will likely continue to penetrate a wide variety of other equipment categories through the use of integrated chips. Communications technology also is undergoing rapid change, and we are on the verge of commercialization of both nano-technology and genetic technology. One consequence of this multifaceted technological acceleration is the likelihood that an increasing share of production capacity will become economically and competitively obsolete before it becomes functionally obsolete. Clearly, the implication is that we are facing an era in which the strategic importance of capital-asset management will rise quickly. Getting stuck in an older technology may become a major problem not only for individual firms, but for whole industries—or even for entire economies.

Getting stuck in an older technology may become a major problem not only for individual firms, but for whole industries— or even for entire economies.

Hardware is by no means the only focus of concern. Databases, software and networks are the others. Investments in these items are also capital assets in need of management, protection and business integration. Investing in the wrong technology or failing to stay current with change can be deadly. So an organization has to make these asset choices well. Perhaps the most critical asset-management issue relates to the management of human capital. Renowned management theorist Peter Drucker says that the greatest and most valuable body of capital in advanced economies today is the portable type. It is based between the ears of knowledge workers who are highly mobile and have mostly dismissed the concept of company loyalty.

The training, experience and creativity of these people are invaluable. And so we have to begin thinking in terms of attracting, training and keeping the right people as a core part of our capital-expenditure strategy. This will involve distinguishing the human-capital dimension of your business from both traditional personnel issues and traditional capital budgeting methods.

The Capex Driver & Sales Growth

With this broader perspective, let's return to the specific cash-flow dimension of capital expenditures as a cash driver. Management often finds it helpful to measure this cash driver by relating capital expenditures to sales growth. The driver is determined by dividing actual net capital expenditures by sales increase. For example, if last year's sales were $10 million and this year's are $11 million, and the company spent $350,000 on capital items, then the Capex cash driver is \$350,000 ÷ \$1,000,000, or 0.35. A Capex cash driver of 0.35 means that 35 cents out of every dollar of increased sales went into capital expenditures.

Although the calculation answers a particular question, it raises many more that it is not our purpose to answer here. For example: Is \$350,000 enough? What was it for? Does it have any strategic purpose? How are competitors spending their capital-expenditure budgets? Perhaps the most relevant question is, does the calculation cost-effectively advance the company's position relative to competition in the context of its strategic goals? For Tom and Sally Fegley's chocolate business, the tug of war in Capex decision making is between additional production capacity and additional retail space. As the Fegleys shift their distribution-channel mix more toward their own outlets, a whole new set of tactical issues develops in the trade-offs between production and retail, the two very different strategic sides of their company.

Linking the Capex cash driver to sales growth does not mean that growth is the only thing driving Capex. In fact, even with no growth, replacement of fully depreciated and used-up assets is regularly necessary.

Linking the Capex cash driver to sales growth does not mean that growth is the only thing driving Capex. In fact, even with no growth, replacement of fully depreciated and used-up assets is regularly necessary. A simplifying assumption here, in a no-growth scenario, is that ongoing depreciation expense is tied to the useful life of the asset and adequately matches expense to the related revenue. This makes reported profit reasonably accurate. Presumably, then, when the asset is fully depreciated, it is replaced with something that is comparable in terms of both cost and functionality. Ongoing profitability, therefore, would be unchanged by the replacement because depreciation and interest expenses remain about the same for the new unit as for the item that was replaced. This, of course, presumes no inflation and no improvement in price/performance ratio. In reality, there is almost always some level of inflation, just as there is often a price/performance improvement that contributes to greater productivity.

In the real world, the no-growth choice for business is seldom an option except, perhaps, for a one-person operation or closely held family affair that doesn't expect to continue beyond the first generation. For most others, to stand still is to fall further behind one's competition. An enterprise that wants to stay in business must tune in to the capitalist imperative of growth. If it doesn't, its customers will almost certainly drift—flock—to more competitive alternatives.

Better-than-average growth depends on new investment to keep it going. By new investment, I mean equity injections from which everything else can be leveraged to grow as fast as possible without sacrificing the rate of return to owners that justifies attracting additional equity in the first place.

Better-than-average growth depends on new investment to keep it going. By new investment, I mean not just retained earnings from the business or additional debt and trade credit in the same general proportions as in the past. By new investment I mean equity injections from which everything else can be leveraged to grow as fast as possible without sacrificing the rate of return to owners that justifies attracting additional equity in the first place.

Depreciation & Capex

The Capex cash driver of 0.35 in the example above may sound like a high proportion, but remember that the assets acquired have depreciable lives. If a particular asset has a seven-year depreciable life for both tax purposes (IRS depreciation table) and financial reporting (your accountant's judgment), for example, the 0.35 ratio, though fully expended this year, is *expensed* through the process of depreciation at only one-seventh of that per year on average. The cash-flow impact of buying that capital asset is far more negative (by 6 to 1) in cash terms than in profit terms. Actually, it is a little more complicated than that because the depreciation is tax deductible on an accelerated basis, so the difference in cash and profit terms isn't quite as bad as 6 to 1.

Although depreciation is not a cash expense, it is fortunately deductible as an expense for tax purposes. This makes the cash-flow implications of depreciation a little tricky to sort out. For income-statement and income-tax purposes, we use depreciation expense–a way to recover and allocate the original cost of the asset. But for cash-flow purposes, we ignore depreciation per se because it is a noncash cost. For cash-flow purposes, we use actual cash expenditures made when the capital asset was acquired.

For growing companies whose Capex is also growing, deferred taxes become an ongoing source of essentially free capital. Once again, an increase in a liability account is counted as cash in.

It is important to understand that the allocated cost called depreciation is often different for income-statement purposes than it is for tax purposes. You actually have two sets of books. For financial-statement purposes, depreciation is usually pretty much the same year to year for a given set of assets. For income-tax purposes, you depreciate faster—that is, more of the asset's cost is allocated proportionally to the earlier years of its life than to the later years. Since depreciation is an expense, that means more expense and hence less profit in the earlier years. Less profit, of course, means lower taxes—so depreciation acts as a tax shelter. Here's the rub, though. In subsequent years, the size of the shelter shrinks and you wind up with a lower depreciation expense. This translates to more profit and higher taxes in those later years of the asset's depreciable life. Truly, there is no free lunch, except that you did have what amounts to a free loan from the government for a while in an amount equal to the taxes postponed by the use of accelerated depreciation.

This interest-free loan from the government shows up as a liability on your balance sheet in an account called "deferred income taxes payable." There is a very helpful feature of deferred taxes for growing companies if they have an ongoing capital-expenditure pattern that also grows: Their new capital expenditures are typically getting larger, so the interest-free loan keeps getting larger in proportion. This works even though the rate of growth is being moderated by averaging in with older assets, gradually forcing the company into playing some degree of tax payment catch-up with the IRS. The happy result of all this for growing companies whose Capex is also growing is that deferred taxes become an ongoing source of essentially free capital. Once again, an increase in a liability account is counted as cash in.

Leasing & Capex

I n evaluating capital-expenditure options, companies frequently find leasing to be a better deal than buying. A good part of the economic benefit of leasing is attributable to the fact that leasing companies often have more buying leverage, more income to shelter from taxes and a higher tax rate than their customers do. The result is that some of this greater net advantage is passed along to the company that elects to lease rather than buy. As discussed in Chapter 4, you might be able to keep balance-sheet debt lower by leasing. The determination involves many detailed IRS distinctions, but all are rooted essentially in whether the lessor or the lessee bears the primary risks of ownership. Financing-type leases must have the present value of scheduled lease payments shown as a liability on the balance sheet. But operating leases do not have to be reported on the face of the balance sheet.

Capital Budgeting

I n addition to the strategic issues regarding Capex, there are at least two other levels to Capex analysis—screening and selection. Screening is the process of determining whether a proposed Capex investment meets the firm's basic investment criteria. Selection is the harder task of choosing among the various Capex projects that meet initial screening requirements. Effective capital budgeting at both the screening and selection levels has long been one of cash flow's analytical advantages over profitability. There are a couple of worthwhile techniques for capital budgeting, and although it is beyond the scope of this book to present those methodologies, it's worth noting that each is clearly based on measuring and assessing the cash flows involved.

In doing cash-flow-based capital budgeting, there are two particular things worth remembering: depreciation—especially accelerated depreciation as a tax shield—and the concept of after-tax effect. Depreciation as a tax shield is simply based on the noncash nature of depreciation expense when calculating cash flows. So, for example, when you calculate the cash flows in and out resulting from any investment decision, depreciation on a purchased asset never figures into the equation because it is not a cash cost. The concept of the after-tax effect means that an expense that is tax-deductible really doesn't cost what you pay for it; instead, it costs what you pay less the taxes you save on the higher profit you would have reported without the expense. So, for example, the interest portion of your mortgage payment this month doesn't really cost you the $1,000 that you pay the bank. Instead, it costs you $1,000 minus, say, $380 tax savings created by a 31% tax rate on your federal return and 7% on your state income-tax return. That is how much higher your taxes would be if you didn't have the mortgage-interest deduction.

> **In doing cash-flow-based capital budgeting, there are two particular things worth remembering: depreciation—especially accelerated depreciation as a tax shield—and the concept of after-tax effect.**

Capex & Growth

For companies at the low- or no-growth level, capital expenditures are little more than a replacement exercise, even though some technological evolution is usually involved. Where significant growth is actively pursued through positive net capital-expenditure planning and spending, the task becomes more challenging. Most growing businesses go through a cycle in which growth accelerates, then slows, then plateaus. The cycle may not be repeated, but it is a common pattern. Over the full cycle, the need for capital expansion and the ability to fund it internally move perversely in opposite directions.

At the peak of growth acceleration, a company's need for space, equipment and development is usually greatest. Yet that is precisely when the demand for cash to fund additional working assets leaves the least cash available for anything else. Conversely, when growth does plateau, there is ordinarily much more cash available. Over a several-year period, perhaps matching the likely growth cycle, lenders ordinarily want to see significant cumulative cash projected on the cash-after-debt amortization line of the cash-flow statement. Significant enough, that is, to represent some sort of reasonable down-payment percentage relative to projected capital expenditures over the same period. The steeper or more erratic the growth cycle, the more difficult it gets to convince a lender that this is a deal worth doing. Obviously this puts a premium on finding ways to blunt some of the cycle's extremes. The basic choices are to either moderate the growth cycle or to attempt to offset its effects.

At the peak of growth acceleration, a company's need for space, equipment and development is usually greatest. Yet that is precisely when the demand for cash to fund additional working assets leaves the least cash available for anything else.

Looking first at trying to offset some of the growth cycle's effects, you may find that short-term leasing—that is, operating leases of needed additional assets—is an appealing option. There is a cost premium with this approach compared with either outright purchase or longer-term financing leases. On the other hand, an operating lease avoids risking overcommitment to investment in Capex, in case growth should subsequently slow more quickly than expected. The outsourcing of some services, or the subcontracting of functions that are normally provided from internal sources, can also serve to reduce your exposure to overcommitment risk. That risk reduction applies to overcommitment in both Capex and people investments. Again, there is usually a cost premium to these shorter-term rental or outsourcing solutions, but there's also a significant reduction in risk.

Direct efforts to smooth out peaks of the growth cycle can also be a fertile field for minimizing the risk of overinvestment in additional capacity. Here you want to look for manageable ways to segment your market's total demand without undue risk of losing or shrinking it. If your marketplace can be segmented geographically and the segments approached sequentially, the growth peak may be moderated. A major trade-off risk, of course, might be giving your competition more response time than you are comfortable with. Even so, the total mix of benefits from a smoother but longer growth cycle may be worth the competitive risk. Do the homework. List the pros and cons. Pencil out the likely scenarios, then turn them into alternative forecasts to be compared with one another. In fact, this process of alternative scenario analysis is the heart of the cash-driver shaping and projections process that we turn to next.

Cash Flow & Business Management

The Mechanics of Cash-Driver Shaping & Projections

HIS CHAPTER WILL SHOW HOW AN IN-DEPTH historical analysis of your business in cash-flow and cash-driver terms can help you shape a vision for where you are headed. From a business point of view, the primary value of historical data is as a source of information for plotting trend lines into the future. This forward view is often a different perspective from the one your accountant may be used to providing. Many accountants become so focused on accurately describing what has happened, according to generally accepted accounting principles, that they do not focus as much as you may need on the forward view. Although I would never advocate throwing away your rearview mirror, neither would I recommend using it to replace your windshield. The forward look is the essence of this and the remaining chapters of this book.

We'll revisit the cash drivers using an extended and detailed hypothetical case study that illustrates how to influence the drivers on an integrated basis as you move your company forward. The output of this integrating-thought process will produce a set of likely future cash-driver values (the cash driver shaping sheet—CDSS) that can then be converted to projected cash-flow statements to reveal the cash consequences of the strategies embedded in the CDSS assumptions. The chapter is about these two things. Let me restate them for clarity:

- **shaping the cash-driver values for coming periods** in the context of the specific business issues of a particular company; and

■ **going through the necessary mechanical steps** to turn those values into an actual cash-flow forecast. We will do that on a line-by-line basis, using as a guide for format the Uniform Credit Analysis®, (UCA) cash-flow worksheet recommended in Chapter 4 (and reprinted on pages 180-181). Some readers may want to postpone or skip this chapter because it's more detailed than is either necessary or appropriate for their current job. Others may prefer to use their own business dynamics as the crucible for thinking contextually about the seven cash drivers and then turning them into a projected cash-flow statement. Everyone else, please prepare to dive right in.

Shaping the Cash Drivers

If forecasting the cash drivers begins with a look at where they were in the past, you first must decide how far back to look. I recommend a three-to-five-year time horizon. Three years is the minimum needed to provide basic trend insights and identify elements with greater apparent variability. Five years is probably as far back as is either relevant or retrievable. The further back you go, the less readily and accurately you can describe the underlying business realities that shaped the cash drivers.

In addition to the cash drivers, short- and long-term interest rates need to be quickly forecast. You need to have a rate at which to price any additional debt that your projected cash flow indicates will be necessary. You can forecast this interest rate fairly safely by using rates that reflect the current market. Then carry them forward unchanged unless you have some particular insight for changing them.

Let's start by looking at a cash-driver shaping sheet (CDSS) for our hypothetical (but based loosely on reality) case study, National Transaction Technology Corp. (See the box at the top of the next page). NTTC is a potential $38 million sales consolidation of several smaller printers around the country who are evaluating participation in a roll-up under the leadership of an appropriately experienced executive to be recruited as CEO. Although they have not yet been rolled up, we have put their

---

BOX 12-1	**Cash Driver Shaping Sheet (CDSS)**						

National Transaction Technology Corp.

	'97	'98	'99	'00	'01	'02	'03
Sales growth %	2	2	1	3	—	—	—
Gross margin % (excluding depreciation)	48	47	46	43	—	—	—
SG&A % (excluding depreciation)	37	38	39	40	—	—	—
Cushion % (GM-SG&A)	11	9	7	3			
A/R in days	29	31	31	31	—	—	—
Inventory in days	50	49	49	47	—	—	—
Payables in days	39	38	37	40	—	—	—
Capex net $ (in thousands)	0	0	0	0	—	—	—
Short-term interest rate %					8.5	8.5	8.5
Long-term interest rate %					10	10	10

---

financials and CDSS ratios together on an as-if-rolled-up basis for purposes of analysis. The partner companies will continue their own local marketing and customer-service operations, selling primarily to credit unions and community banks. They will also continue their own local operations aside from Magnetic Ink Character Recognition (MICR), the special character and magnetic ink printing used on checks and some other specialized financial documents. Centralizing production of the non-MICR operations offers little advantage at present. The companies will, however, integrate their higher-volume MICR production and shipping facilities in a state-of-the-art facility in Kansas City. The increase in fixed costs for that facility will be almost exactly offset by lower direct labor costs for the next three years. At that point, the labor-cost savings should begin to outstrip the fixed-cost differential by about three quarters of a full point of sales in each of the next several years.

One of the main things drawing the group together is recognition that the conventional check-printing business (about 60% of the combined total sales volume) is slowing rapidly. Industry growth is expected to turn negative in the next few years as various electronic and card-based payment mechanisms continue to expand, most especially through Internet-based bill payment. The roll-up partners feel a need to get ahead of the big three market leaders in the MICR check and related-forms business, while they stake out a position or niche in the higher-technology areas of the payments business.

Imagine yourself coming into this situation as a CEO interviewee. The rest of the team is well organized with good relationships and mutual respect. These relationships have developed from years of working together in the same industry and sharing information in common against the big three check producers with whom they have all individually competed. There is a good deal of confidence in you as the search team's top preliminary choice. The financials on which your shaping sheet was prepared show a break-even situation for fiscal 2000 on both a cash and accrual basis. In cash terms, the '00 outflows attributable to the erosion in cushion were almost exactly offset by the cash inflows associated with fewer days inventory and a bit more in days payable. This is a classic case of using tighter management of the swing factors to offset erosion in the fundamentals. Some other key ratios for '00 are:

Current ratio: Current assets over current liabilities = 1.58
Leverage: Total liabilities over total net worth = 0.45
Asset efficiency: Sales over total assets = 1:36

All things considered, this is neither a great nor a terrible situation. You decide that the first thing you need to do in determining whether to leave your present position is to think through the questions relevant to the cash drivers for at least the next three years and see what they lead to in cash terms. Since we are doing this manually for illustrative purposes, we will project only one year out. Let's take a look now at the cash drivers in our standard sequence.

Sales Growth

You need to determine the answers to three key questions regarding sales growth.

WHAT'S HAPPENING IN THE MAIN PRODUCT LINE OF CHECK PRINTING; HOW WILL IT/CAN IT/SHOULD IT AFFECT SALES VOLUME FOR THAT SEGMENT IN THE NEXT THREE YEARS?

After some discussion with key sales managers in several regions of the country, you conclude that you will almost certainly lose at least some business, ostensibly on price, to some of the bigger producers. But even if you matched them on price, you would likely lose some sales anyway. The reason is that reopening of the periodic bid process is being driven mostly by banking-industry consolidation. The consolidator banks already tend to be customers of the major producers. Those consolidating banks that do stay with you, with or without reopening of bids, will stay more because of your service and responsiveness than for price reasons. You conclude from all this that your best reasonable goal for the next few years will be to target a move of your growth rate up to 5% in the check business. Two-thirds of that increase you expect to come from unit volume increases due to more efficient and intensive territory coverage. An apparently well-thought-out plan has already been put together for sales-force integration. The balance of check-printing growth is expected to come from slight price increases in bid situations where you have a particular service-quality edge, as well as in market areas where consolidation seems to have slowed.

WHAT ABOUT THE OTHER EXISTING SEGMENTS?

You see a healthy diversity of specialties in the variety of other business segments and lines represented by NTTC's various regional operators. These include some mundane and routine types of business, as well as a few having significant market or product edges over competitors. These latter compose a third of the group. The sales-force integration plan has already established assignments, training, pricing and promotional plans to build on the places where there are particular strengths and to let the more mundane end of the business be driven by a move to be the low-cost producer. General printing, 40% of the total present business, is targeting increased growth as the new marketing plan is implemented at levels of 8%, 15%, and 20% in '01, '02 and '03. Gross margins and SG&A in general printing have been indistinguishable from those in the total company.

WHAT NEW IS COMING ALONG, AND WHAT ARE THE POTENTIAL EFFECTS?
Negotiations are almost complete on a licensing agreement to
market a line of PC-driven MICR printers and a franchise-support
port system to small, local entrepreneurs. The franchisees will
sell personalized check products to consumer households as
fundraisers through high schools, service clubs and hospital aux-
iliaries. This will put NTTC into the consumer check business
for the first time, since virtually all its existing check-printing volume has been business-related. NTTC is being offered a three
year marketing exclusive within a 200-mile radius of each of its
14 locations around the country. Part of the appeal lies in the
franchise MICR business on its own, and the other part in its
contractual relationship with an Internet bill-payment consor-
tium that involves several top-tier banking organizations.

After weighing all the input, you conclude that as a strictly
pass-through marketing operation, the franchise MICR business will take virtually no inventory, payables or accounts
receivable. Gross margins look very close to your recent companywide average, and SG&A is proportionally about half what
you have been running. The sales forecasts for 2001, 2002 and
2003 are $1,400,000, $5,800,000 and $13,000,000, respectively.
Getting started up will take about $1,400,000, which you will
capitalize and amortize over five years. Putting it all together
yields the following:

Sales Growth Forecast Summary

	'01	'02	'03
Check printing: (60% of $38m sales x 0.05 annual growth yields sales in millions)	$23.94	$25.14	$26.4
General printing: (40% of $38m sales x 0.08, 0.15 , & 0.20 annual growth yields sales in millions)	$16.42	$18.88	$22.65
MICR franchise (in millions)	$1.4	$5.8	$13.0
Total sales forecasted (in millions)	$41.76	$49.82	$62.05
Total growth rate over prior year	9.9%	19.3%	24.5%

Gross Margin

You have already seen most of the observations affecting gross margin within the sales-growth discussion. There is one major exception—the general printing category. As prospective CEO, you pose appropriate questions, and further analysis is undertaken. Subsequent conversation with key people suggests that price increases on the niche side of that business will about match the job-cost reductions on the more routine side—averaging about 1.75% overall margin improvement from last year's total company average and likely continuing at that higher level for several years. Let's summarize all this:

Gross Margin Weighted Average Summary
(percentages of sales)

	'01	'02	'03
Check printing	24.7%	21.7%	18.3%
General printing	17.6	17.0	16.4
Franchise MICR	1.4	5.0	9.0
Companywide gross margin	43.7	43.7	43.7

Note that even with all things considered and factored in, there is no difference in overall gross margin across the entire projection period. This is despite the significant shift in business mix reflected in the weighted averages above. If you looked at contribution margin, you almost certainly would find a different story, because the small but growing franchise MICR business has a much lower than average SG&A component. Let's focus now on that SG&A component.

Selling General & Administrative Expense

It turns out that there simply is not adequate time in your recruitment timetable as prospective CEO to explore this area in any depth. You conclude from discussions, however, that since there is no compelling reason to change projected SG&A percent from the current level, you will change it only to reflect the separability of the franchise MICR business and its inherently lower (by half) SG&A level. The resultant companywide SG&A percent can be seen in the table below:

Weighted Average SG&A Component by Line
(percentage of sales)

	'01	'02	'03
Printing	38.9%	35.3%	31.6%
Franchise MICR	0.7	2.3	4.2
Company-wide SG&A	39.6	37.6	35.8

If the assumptions about lower SG&A in the franchising business, as compared with the printing business, are correct (there is some rather good supporting data), then the total company SG&A cash driver should improve as the sales mix shifts per the sales forecast. The net result is that this driver alone will improve cushion (gross margin minus SG&A) by 3.8% between '01 and '03.

Accounts Receivable

There is no reasonable expectation of change in accounts-receivable days in the check-printing business. With general printing, however, NTTC has two things going for it: a lower-cost strategy for the more routine business, and a niche-marketing approach in the specialty areas. These factors will enable NTTC to improve averages significantly for both order size and client size. That should make the work flow in that A/R section more efficient, provide for more intense coverage of the accounts, and permit more up-front client credit screening and appropriate setting of credit limits. As prospective CEO, you expect the net result of these improvements to cut about a half day from total A/R days in 2001, and a full day in 2002 and 2003; the growth of franchise MICR (requiring near-zero investment in accounts receivable) will add another expected improvement of a half day in 2001, two days in 2002 and three in 2003. The net of all this for the company, then, is:

Forecasted A/R Days

'01	'02	'03
30	28	27

Inventory & Accounts Payable

NTTC has no particular reason to believe that either inventory days or payables days will change from the most recent year in its existing business lines. The new franchise MICR line of business will have the effect of reducing inventory and payables days for the company as a whole because, by itself, the franchise business model requires neither inventory nor payables. The overall result will be a companywide reduction of one, three and six days respectively in each of the next three years for both inventory and payables.

	'01	'02	'03
Days payable	39	37	34
Days inventory	46	44	41

Capital Expenditures

The forecast for Capex can be done either in terms of some relative measure, as is usually best in a large, diversified company, or simply in absolute dollars for a smaller and simpler business. NTTC falls in between these descriptions because, although it is a fairly simple business, it has 14 locations. These have a mix of equipment types, age, condition, capacities and specializations. In some cases facilities are owned, and in others they are leased. Because of some deterioration in the fundamentals of the business over the past several years, it may well be that the rate of capital expenditure has been unduly light. Let's take a look.

Over the past four years, annual sales growth has averaged only about 2%, with total growth for the four years at only 8%. Say that half the growth was due to inflation and half was real. Over a four-year period, net capital expenditures might have been expected to bear some positive relationship to sales growth, but there has been none. There were no net capital expenditures over those four years. That suggests that the real unit volume growth of about 4% was absorbed with the same aging fixed-asset base. That is not particularly surprising. The business may have been operating at well under capacity, given the slow growth and softness in margins.

Going forward, NTTC has committed to $1,400,000 in start-up expenses to be capitalized—that is, amounts booked as assets rather than expense, then written off over five years. As CEO, you would handle that effectively as a capital expense in '01 for the franchise MICR opportunity. Additionally, you assume implementation of the plant manager's recommendation of $2,850,000 worth of new equipment to become a low-cost producer in the routine end of the general printing business. The final piece for Capex is based on your observations that NTTC's facilities and equipment are generally less than up-to-date. Consequently, you assume that about half the anticipated sales-growth rate in real terms (everything above 2%) should be added to gross furniture, fixtures, equipment and buildings. This is annual net ongoing Capex in addition to the already mentioned $1,400,000 and $2,850,000 pieces. Here is how this all works out:

Capex (in thousands)

	'01	'02	'03
Franchise MICR startup	$1,400		
Low-cost producer equip.	2,850		
General Capex	$2,800	$3,200	$7,800
Total Capex	$7,050	$3,200	$7,800

Now that the first-pass forecast of cash drivers is finished, enter all of them for the next three years onto the cash-driver shaping sheet that we began filling with the historical data on page 165. The box at the top of the next page shows the completed shaping sheet.

Projecting Future Cash Flows

Armed with the figures from the cash-driver shaping sheet (CDSS), we can project future cash flows. We begin by applying the CDSS assumptions for the year 2001 to NTTC's income statement for 2000 (page 174), along with 2000's ending balance sheet (page 176). In the discussion in Chapter 4, we explained that we needed a starting and

---

BOX 12-2 | **Cash Driver Shaping Sheet (CDSS)**

National Transaction Technology Corp.

	'97	'98	'99	'00	'01	'02	'03
Sales growth %	2	2	1	3	9.9	19.3	24.5
Gross margin % (excluding depreciation)	48	47	46	43	43.7	43.7	43.7
SG&A % (excluding depreciation)	37	38	39	40	39.6	37.6	35.8
Cushion % (GM-SG&A)	11	9	7	3	4.1	6.1	7.9
A/R in days	29	31	31	31	30	28	27
Inventory in days	50	49	49	47	46	44	41
Payables in days	39	38	37	40	39	37	34
Capex net $ (in thousands)	0	0	0	0	7,050	3,200	7,800
Short-term interest rate %					8.5	8.5	8.5
Long-term interest rate %					10	10	10

ending balance sheet, along with the intervening period's income statement to fill in the cash-flow worksheet. Now that we are doing a projected cash-flow statement, the projection itself will serve as the income statement as we create it. We will also be forecasting the needed elements of the ending balance sheet as we go. With those pieces, we can construct a projected cash-flow statement for 2001 in the UCA cash-adjusted income-statement format, then use the 2001 figures and assumptions for 2002, and so on. This future cash-flow projection for the NTTC roll-up is found on page 178.

Let's first consider a few examples of how we go from the last year of historical data to a first year of cash-flow projection by applying forecasted CDSS driver assumptions. We begin with year 2000 actual sales of $38,188,000 from the income statement and apply the sales-growth forecast of 9.9% from the CDSS to get forecasted 2001 sales of $41,968,612 (2000 sales x 1.099).

Next on the cash-flow projection, we need to adjust that projected 2001 sales figure for the change in accounts receivable in order to find projected cash from sales. The year-end

BOX 12-3	**NTTC Income Statement 2000**	
Net sales		$38,188,000
Cost of goods sold		21,767,160
Depreciation in cost of goods sold		763,760
GROSS PROFIT/REVENUES		**$ 15,657,080**
Sales, general & administrative expenses (SG&A)		15,275,200
Depreciation		384,000
TOTAL OPERATING EXPENSES		**$ 15,659,200**
OPERATING PROFIT		**(2,120)**
Other income		267,932
EBITDA (earnings before interest, taxes, depreciation & amortization)		**$ 1,413,572**
EBIT (earnings before interest & taxes)		**$ 265,812**
Total interest expense		
		267,325
PROFIT BEFORE TAXES & EXTRA ITEMS		**(1,513)**
Current taxes		(367)
PROFIT BEFORE EXTRA ITEMS		**(1,146)**
NET PROFIT		**(1,146)**

2000 balance sheet shows accounts receivable of $3,243,364, which we know (from the CDSS) represented 31 days worth of 2000 sales. But we are forecasting a drop to 30 days of accounts receivable at the end of 2001 and so:

30 ÷ 365 x $41,968,612 (2001's projected sales) =
    $3,449,475 (projected year-end 2001 accounts receivable)

That's an increase of $206,111 from the end of 2000 and represents an additional cash outflow on 2001's cash-flow statement. Note that even though receivables are managed a bit more tightly overall as measured by the drop from 31 days to 30 days, they are still increasing in absolute dollars because of the sales-growth factor.

Next comes cost of goods sold, which is 1 minus gross margin percentage. Stated another way, gross margin is what remains after cost of goods sold is subtracted from sales. Since forecasted gross margin for 2001 on our CDSS is 43.7%, then cost of goods sold must be 1 minus 0.437, or 0.563 of sales. Forecast sales for 2001 of $41,968,612 x 0.563 = $23,628,329 cost of goods sold. That number, too, has to be adjusted for the change in relevant balance-sheet values in order to present it in cash terms—that is, to move from cost of goods sold to cash production costs, which requires that we then calculate projected changes in inventory and payables. As done above with accounts receivable, we have to calculate forecasted values for these payables and inventory figures based on days assumptions captured on the CDSS. Then we indicate the cash effect of the resultant movement up or down, remembering that an increase in a liability (such as payables) is always considered cash in—that is, a positive number in cash terms. An increase in an asset, though, goes the opposite way, the presumption of cash out to increase any asset, in this case, inventory.

In the process of completing the cash-flow projection, we will have to make a few relatively simple and quite reasonable assumptions. At some point, you will probably want to set this up on a computer spreadsheet for real-world use. For purposes of learning and understanding, however, I recommend that you do it manually at least a few times first. Before you go the rest of the way into the line-by-line detail of the projection, it may be helpful to review once more the general sequence of the cash-flow statement logic.

The Logic of Cash Flow

We begin by assuming that everything called sales or revenue is cash coming in and everything of an expense nature is cash going out. Earlier we referred to this as the as-though cash

BOX 12-4 | NTTC Balance Sheet 12/30/2000

ASSETS:

Cash and marketable securities	$1,400,000
Accounts receivable (net)	3,243,364
Inventory	2,802,895
Other current assets	656,200
Current assets	**$ 8,102,459**
Land	3,300,000
All other gross fixed assets	35,400,045
Less: Accumulated depreciation	18,654,356
Fixed assets (net)	**$20,045,689**
TOTAL ASSETS	**$28,148,148**

LIABILITIES:

Notes payable short-term (banks & others)	$2,025,091
Debt in current liabilities	**$2,025,091**
Accounts payable	2,385,442
Accruals	516,980
Other current liabilities	212,400
Current liabilities	**$5,139,913**
Long-term debt	3,625,517
Total senior long-term liabilities	**$3,625,517**
TOTAL LIABILITIES	**$8,765,430**

NET WORTH:

Common stock	1,000,000
Retained earnings	18,382,718
TOTAL NET WORTH	**$19,382,718**
TOTAL LIABILITIES & NET WORTH	**$28,148,148**

assumption behind accrual statements. No sooner do we make the as-though assumption for each major line item on the income statement, however, than we immediately back off the assumption and adjust to cash reality. We make that adjustment by adding to or subtracting from the particular income-statement line any change in whichever balance-sheet items most directly relate to that particular line. In several cases we forecast the ending balance-sheet values directly, as with receivables, inventory and payables, based on our assessment of their movement in days. Capex is probably easiest to deal with as a direct-dollar forecast based on specific or likely plans. In other cases, where there is no explicit basis on which to make a forecast of projected values, it is generally wise to forecast based on applying a growth rate to whatever last year's value was—typically the rate of sales growth also represents a reasonable surrogate for growth of these other items. We do this, for example, with prepaid expenses and accrued expenses. We do it as well with the categories bundled into miscellaneous as in Step V below.

The mechanics of the plus-or-minus adjustment process for balance-sheet data are simple if you remember the basic rules: Increases in assets imply cash flowing out, that is, cash minuses; and increases in liabilities imply cash flowing in, cash pluses. Sales or revenue imply cash flowing in; expenses imply cash flowing out. In each case, of course, the opposites hold as well. Take a moment now and refer to the cash-flow worksheet on pages 180-181, and work through the logic flow described here in terms of the steps on the worksheet.

The UCA cash-flow report for NTTC on page 178 lays out the results of the mechanics of this process that we began to work through above in the first several examples. Most of it is quite logical. The following ten steps outline the process for completing the basic UCA cash-flow worksheet (pages 180-181). You may want to review the steps as you track the completed NTTC report, then use it to complete a cash-flow projection for your business. (In the calculations that follow, the * means the value of the item less any depreciation that may be included in it.)

I. Sales plus or minus the change in A/R equals cash from sales

BOX 12-5	UCA, Cash Flow Report NTTC Roll-Up		
	Forecast 2001	Forecast 2002	Forecast 2003
Sales (net)	$41,968,612	$50,068,554	$62,335,350
Change in receivables	(206,111)	(391,400)	(770,233)
Cash from sales	**41,762,501**	**49,677,154**	**61,565,117**
Cost of goods sold	(23,628,329)	(28,188,596)	(35,094,802)
Change in inventories	(174,922)	(420,261)	(544,079)
Change in payables	139,229	332,803	411,631
Cash production costs	**(23,664,022)**	**(28,276,053)**	**(35,227,250)**
Gross cash profits	**18,098,479**	**21,401,101**	**26,337,867**
SG&A expense	(16,619,570)	(18,825,776)	(22,316,055)
Changes in accruals	51,181	109,655	166,065
Misc. transactions	250,521	257,154	294,795
Cash operating expense	**(16,317,868)**	**(18,458,967)**	**(21,855,195)**
Cash after operations	**1,780,611**	**2,942,134**	**4,482,672**
Income taxes paid	——	367	(240,011)
Net cash after operations	**1,780,611**	**2,942,501**	**4,242,661**
Interest expense	(924,873)	(1,354,488)	(1,751,908)
Financing costs	**(924,873)**	**(1,354,488)**	**(1,751,908)**
Net cash income	**855,738**	**1,588,013**	**2,490,753**
Cash after debt amortization	**855,738**	**1,588,013**	**2,490,753**
Capital expenditures-tangible	**(7,050,000)**	**(3,200,000)**	**(7,800,000)**
CASH AFTER Capital spending	**(6,194,262)**	**(1,611,987)**	**(5,309,247)**
Financing SURPLUS/(requirement)	**(6,194,262)**	**(1,611,987)**	**(5,309,247)**
Change in short-term debt	6,315,414	1,867,723	5,702,177
Total external financing	**6,315,414**	**1,867,723**	**5,702,177**
Cash after financing	**121,152**	**255,736**	**392,931**
Actual change in cash	**121,152**	**255,736**	**392,931**
Net income + Depreciation	1,090,664	2,129,699	3,291,210

II. Less: cost of goods sold*, or cost of sales,* plus-or-minus changes in inventory and payables, to arrive at cash production (or acquisition) costs. These in turn are subtracted from your cash-from-sales figure to get gross cash margins.

III. Next, adjust SG&A expense* for plus-and-minus changes in prepaid assets and accrued expenses to get cash operating expense.

IV. Gross cash margins (from Step II) less cash operating expense (from Step III) leaves cash from operations.

V. Now adjust for all miscellaneous-category pluses and minuses as appropriate to get the net change in all of the other categories: other income and expense, changes in other assets and other liabilities. Cumulatively call this miscellaneous cash income (or expense).

VI. Then come income taxes: provision for taxes from the income statement is adjusted for all plus-and-minus changes in balance-sheet accounts that are income-tax related to arrive at cash taxes paid.

Summarizing: Cash from operations (Step IV), plus or minus miscellaneous cash income (Step V), plus or minus cash taxes paid (Step VI) leaves net cash from operations.

At this point you have net cash from operations, but what you don't yet have is cash from financing and cash from investing. These three categories of cash flow—operating, financing and investing—are what the American Institute of CPAs (AICPA) requires as part of its directive on the subject of cash flow. So far, you have gotten only to the operating level; now you can proceed to the remaining two categories. You will do it in a way that creates some of the key summary lines that both you and your banker will need to know.

VII. Net cash income is calculated from net cash from operations at step six and adjusted, plus and minus, for interest and dividend expenses. It is adjusted as well for changes in related balance-sheet accounts such as interest payable and dividends payable.

(continued on page 182)

BOX 12-6	**Uniform Credit Analysis® Cash-Flow Worksheet**

ACCOUNT TITLE	LOCATION	CASH IMPACT	
I. Sales	Income statement	(+)	$ _____
Accounts receivable	Balance sheet	decrease (+), increase (-)	_____
Cash from sales			_____
II. Cost of goods sold (COGS)	Income statement	(-)	_____
Depreciation in COGS*	Income statement	(+)	_____
Inventory	Balance sheet	decrease (+), increase (-)	_____
Accounts payable	Balance sheet	increase (+), decrease (-)	_____
Cash production costs			_____
Cash from sales − Cash production costs= **Gross cash profit**			_____
III. Selling, General & Administrative Expense (SG&A)	Income statement	(-)	_____
Depreciation & amortization in SG&A*	Income statement	(+)	_____
Prepaids & deposits	Balance sheet	decrease (+), increase (-)	_____
Accrued liabilities	Balance sheet	increase (+), decrease (-)	_____
Cash Operating Expenses			_____
IV. Gross cash profit − Cash operating expenses = **Cash after operations**			_____
V. Other income	Income statement	(+)	_____
Other expenses	Income statement	(-)	_____
Other current assets	Balance sheet	decrease (+), increase (-)	_____
Other current liabilities	Balance sheet	increase (+), decrease (-)	_____
Other assets	Balance sheet	decrease (+), increase (-)	_____
Other liabilities	Balance sheet	increase (+), decrease (-)	_____
Miscellaneous cash income/expenses			_____
VI. Tax provision (benefit)	Income statement	benefit (+), provision (-)	_____
Income tax refund receivable	Balance sheet	decrease (+), increase (-)	_____
Deferred tax benefit (asset)	Balance sheet	decrease (+), increase (-)	_____
Income taxes payable	Balance sheet	increase (+), decrease (-)	_____
Deferred taxes payable	Balance sheet	increase (+), decrease (-)	_____
Cash taxes paid			_____
Cash after operations + Miscellaneous cash income ÷ expenses + Cash taxes paid = **Net cash after operations**			_____

VII. Interest expense   Income statement   (-)

Dividends or owners'   Income statement   (-)   _____
withdrawal

Dividends payable   Balance sheet   increase (+), decrease (-)   _____

Financing costs   _____

   Net cash after operations – Financing costs = **Net cash income**   _____

VIII. Current maturities   Balance sheet   (-)   _____
long-term debt (prior year)

Current capital lease   Balance sheet   (-)   _____
obligation (prior year)

Scheduled debt amortization   _____

   Net cash income – Scheduled debt amortization = **Cash after debt amortization**   _____

IX. Fixed assets, net   Balance sheet   decrease (+), increase (-)   _____

Intangibles   Balance sheet   decrease (+), increase (-)   _____

Depreciation and   Income statement   (-)   _____
amortization*

Capital spending, net   _____

Investment   Balance sheet   decrease (+), increase (-)   _____

Total capital spending and investment, net   _____

   Cash after debt amortization – Total capital spending
and investment, net = **Financing requirement**   _____

X. Short-term debt   Balance sheet   increase (+), decrease (-)   _____

Long-term debt   Balance sheet   increase (+), decrease (-)   _____
(excluding prior year's current maturities)

Preferred stock   Balance sheet   increase (+), decrease (-)   _____

Common stock   Balance sheet   increase (+), decrease (-)   _____

Paid in capital   Balance sheet   increase (+), decrease (-)   _____

Treasury stock   Balance sheet   decrease (+), increase (-)   _____

Total Financing   _____

   Financing requirement – Total financing = Calculated change in cash   _____

Cash & equivalent   Balance sheet   increase (+), decrease (-)   _____

Marketable securities   Balance sheet   increase (+), decrease (-)   _____

Actual change in cash   _____

   Calculated change in cash = **Actual change in cash**   _____

* Note: Where necessary details regarding depreciation and amortization are not provided on the face of the income statement, you may have to refer to footnotes and/or the statement of changes if provided.

Net cash income tells you whether the company can cover all of its operating expenses and increases in working capital from internally generated sources.

VIII. Cash after debt amortization is derived by reducing net cash income by any repayment of principal on debt. Pick up such repayment from the sum of changes in current maturities of long-term debt and any changes in the current portion of capital-lease obligations. The resultant cash-after-debt-amortization figure tells whether the company can pay scheduled debt from internally generated cash sources. On average, over a few years' time, cash after debt amortization ought to be a positive enough number to represent something of a reasonable proportional down payment on what comes next—that is, capital expenditures and investment.

IX. From cash after debt amortization, you need to subtract all capital expenditures and investment. That will leave you with the total financing requirement for the period. To get capital expenditures, combine all depreciation and amortization expense with any changes in net fixed assets and intangibles. The investment figure is simply the change in the investment category from the balance sheet.

X. Assume that the financing requirement has to be met with additional debt. As a consequence, use the CDSS values for the interest rate to calculate interest expense on the additional debt. Then redo your cash-flow statement from step VII (financing cost) to be sure you are picking up not only the interest on the additional debt but also the additional cost of the interest on that interest.

Putting It All Together

By following the ten steps through with respect to NTTC for the next three years based on your assumptions about the most likely cash-driver values, we arrive at the cash-flow statements on page 178. Note that in 2002 and 2003 net cash income is significantly positive but not nearly positive enough to cover anticipated capital expenditures. There is, however, a reasonable relationship between net cash income and capital expenditures such that the one conceptually represents a reasonable "downpayment" on the other. Presumably then, when the capital-expenditure plan required to change company strategy is completed at the end of the three-year period, continuing growth in positive net-cash income will permit paying off the required debt in a few years This is especially likely to be so, assuming that the strengthened cushion levels continue and that the sales-growth rate begins to moderate a bit—perhaps back to the 15% level. As a prospective CEO, I would conclude that the company has a viable future for remaking itself and significantly increasing shareholder value without undue cash-flow risk—if I have the skill to manage as much change as seems likely to be required.

Cash Drivers &
Strategic Thinking

S WE HAVE SEEN, HYPERACTIVE SALES GROWTH IS one of the most common ways to run out of cash. Others include offering deep price cuts just to keep sales volume up; offering payment terms that are too lenient or too loosely managed; overstocking inventory or investing more in new plants or equipment than can be effectively and efficiently used right away; and consistently paying suppliers early or failing to negotiate with them strongly enough when needed.

There are dozens of things that can affect and shape an enterprise's cash flow. There are also dozens of techniques and methodologies for strategic business planning. This book is intended to sharpen and clarify your thinking by focusing on cash flow through the seven key drivers that dominate it. This chapter focuses on helping you use cash-driver thinking in an integrated way to test the impact of different business alternatives at a conceptual level.

To think strategically about the cash drivers means you must think in terms of potential for business change. With regard to sales growth, it means thinking simultaneously about what is going on inside the firm and in the marketplace for the company's products or services. Next, you put those thoughts into the context of the larger economy in which it all takes place. If there are no relevant changes expected in any of these areas, sales growth is likely to stay about where it has been. But perhaps there is a planned change in the product line, a change that is expected to address some of last year's market-share slippage. Maybe, too, there is an expectation of declining interest rates, and since your business happens to sell primarily to the construction industry, prospects might be very much stronger than last year for sales growth. How much stronger? Someone in your organization has to estimate. Someone has to be able to convert impressions, expectations and calculations into a number, or a range of numbers, defining projected sales growth. With that number in hand, you can now start to construct a projected cash-flow statement for the coming period.

The task of forecasting cash flow can be simplified by making the temporary assumption that all or at least most of the other cash drivers stay constant in relative terms.

The task of forecasting cash flow can be simplified by making the temporary assumption that all or at least most of the other cash drivers stay constant in relative terms. That is, gross margin, SG&A expense, levels of receivables, inventory and payables, and the rate of capital expenditure remain proportionally unchanged. If they do all stay the same as last year, then you can project cash flow based on the change in sales growth alone. Simply work through the ten steps of preparing the projected cash-flow statement (see pages 180-181), and go to the net cash–income line. The difference between net cash–income on a projected basis and its value from last year's actual cash-flow statement will tell you the price tag, in cash, of attaining your sales-growth target.

With that number in hand, you can do some comparison shopping for alternatives as to how you might better use that cash. You can do this by pricing out a range of other possible changes in any other cash driver. Simply recalculate a projected cash-flow statement based on the new assumption about any one of the cash drivers. The main benefit of changing just one cash driver at a time is to get a feel for the relative cash impact that each driver has on your business.

In reality, you will find that a significant change in any one cash driver usually has some interrelated impacts on one or more of the other drivers that you need to reflect in your plan. By starting with just one variable at a time, however, you develop a cash sensitivity reflective of your company's current environment. You may discover, for example, that a three-day change in accounts receivable is roughly equivalent in cash impact to one full point of gross-margin shift, which in turn has about the same cash effect as a 25% difference in your recent Capex budget levels. With such cash sensitivities in mind, you can think more creatively and quickly about the approximate trade-offs under a variety of business alternatives.

In reality, you will find that a significant change in any one cash driver usually has some interrelated impacts on one or more of the other drivers that you need to reflect in your plan.

If you calculate that 12% sales growth is going to cost $1 million in cash, you have a basis on which to ask whether perhaps some other use of that money would be a better strategic buy. You might put the money instead into a production-robotics project that could eventually cut manufacturing costs by 30%. This strategy holds promise of keeping your company competitive in the face of the growing numbers of inexpensive-imports from lower-wage countries. It also opens up another strategic possibility regarding pricing. For example, if you decide on the robotics project instead of sales growth, would it then be possible to be a little less aggressive in cutting your pricing? Without the pressure for sales growth, you won't have to sharpen your pricing pencil quite as much because you are willing to walk away from a few deals. If so, then the resultant point or two of improved margins might be banked for the future just in case your foreign competitors further widen their labor-cost advantage.

There are alternative scenarios that might be evaluated. For example, instead of converting the reduced pressure for sales growth into slightly higher margins through price increases, you might consider offering more lenient credit terms to attract some of the newer and more innovative entrants in your customer field. Easier credit terms would probably be more significant to these younger firms than lower price and thereby represent a better cash use for you. There are many other possibilities. Cash-driver thinking is strategic thinking. Strategic thinking without cash-flow thinking is incomplete at best and disastrous at worst.

Cash-Driver Harmony

The seven cash drivers, taken together, represent a model for viewing your company as a whole because all of the important business issues can be expressed in one or more of the cash drivers. You might think of this cash-driver mindset as the planning palette from which the enterprise artist selects the basic colors of the business scenario. Like a painting, the scenario that works best will have a certain consistency and harmony to it. Certain combinations will tend to go well together, while others simply won't. This isn't to stifle creativity, but simply to recognize that unusual combinations tend to work only when the overall context, the whole picture, will support, and be supportable by, those unusual combinations.

Consider an example of one such combination. If you put together a cash-driver strategy consisting of reducing inventory days and improving profit margins by means of a broadened product line, you have a "color clash." Here's why. A broadened product line automatically implies relatively more inventory, not less. But assume that your business planning has already ruled out being able to do much with any of the other cash drivers. You will have to make the scenario work some other way. What are some ways you might manage to resist the natural tendency toward an increase in inventory days as you add new products and attempt to improve gross margin? Here are some options:

- **redesign the product line or production process to reduce the number of parts or the number of manufacturing steps;**
- **import some of the particularly labor-intensive subassemblies from lower-wage sources;**
- **negotiate with suppliers on faster delivery and smaller order quantities;**

■ **raise minimum-order quantity to be shipped to customers; and**
■ **speed up order processing and shipping times.**

Each of these approaches offers an opportunity to keep relative inventory levels down even as a broadened product line wants to push it up. Each solution, of course, comes with its own mix of issues and costs. Evaluating and managing these alternatives are clearly a lot of work. To move very much further in this particular case, it would be necessary to get into a set of questions and details that exceed the scope of this book. The point here is how thinking in terms of the seven cash drivers can help organize and focus managers' scenario formulations and thought processes on their major business issues. Further, those cash-driver choices are sensitive to and reflective of the most basic of the entity's vital signs—cash flow.

Cash Drivers & Competitive Advantage

Thus far, the discussion of the cash drivers in a strategic sense has focused on the evaluation of alternative strategic cash uses and testing for appropriateness of fit between and among the cash drivers. Let's now take a step back and look more broadly at issues on a higher strategic level. The main such area is competitive advantage.

As you consider your most immediate and likely competitors, you need to be aware of where you stand in terms of relative strengths and weaknesses. If, for example, your competitors have considerably stronger balance sheets than you do, then a strategy that tends to make the business more capital-intensive will probably not be wise. If, on the other hand, you have some advantage in recruiting and training top-notch sales people, a strategy that expands your geographic market area and intensifies sales coverage might have particularly high payback. To the extent that your product or service has any significant proprietary content beyond your competition, investments to further enhance that value or increase the perception of that value in the marketplace might be appropriate. If your track record of union relationships is smoother and more amicable than that of your competitors, a well-constructed plan for increased automation, with some of the benefits going to union members, might considerably improve your long-term competitive position.

In some cases, of course, the competition will have an edge. If your production equipment is older and more limited in terms of sizes or formats of output than that of your competitors, you probably don't want to launch a marketing campaign that unduly emphasizes range of choices. Instead, you might want to identify areas in which you can create some economies associated with the narrower range of choices. The key will always be to maximize cash flow as a return on investment through your decisions in a competitive context. Where can you likely get that return better than the competition? And, how can you avoid getting into competitive positioning situations where others get better cash-flow returns on investment than are available to you?

> **In the future, for all but the most narrowly local firms, foreign-market development will likely become one of the major ways to build shareholder value at anything beyond a merely average rate.**

Cash Drivers & Export Potential

The decision to develop foreign markets is a particularly significant strategic move for any firm, and one that is fraught with both competitive and cash-driver complexity. As our economy becomes ever more globalized, export markets are becoming increasingly important, but foreign competition keeps getting smarter and working harder in our home market. In the future, for all but the most narrowly local firms, foreign-market development will likely become one of the major ways to build shareholder value.

Small and medium-size U.S. firms operating in our large domestic economy are generally at a bit of a disadvantage compared with similar-sized foreign competitors. The sheer size of the American economy is such that many U.S. firms have been able to grow significantly without developing the expertise and flexibility required for the export market. In contrast, many foreign companies have had to develop these capabilities because of the limited size of their home markets. Consequently, they have become stronger, tougher competitors. Too often, American firms fail to pursue the export market in a focused way, but instead approach it haphazardly or opportunistically. While anyone can get lucky, those who do well in developing their export potential are those who do it for the right reasons, with a sound, step-by-step strategy. They do it also from a position of strength, not as a quick fix for problems at home, such as sagging sales, obsolete inventory or eroding margins.

The first issue to consider in evaluating export possibilities is the adequacy of your scarcest resource, management time.

The first issue to consider in evaluating export possibilities is the adequacy of your scarcest resource, management time. Unless your cash drivers are in reasonably good shape overall, you almost certainly can't spare the senior management time that needs to be invested, much of it up front, to develop foreign possibilities. The stronger your cash drivers overall, the greater the probability that you have the depth and breadth of expertise to make it in foreign markets—markets with different practices, where you must accomplish ambitious goals despite the additional obstacles represented by differences of language and culture.

From a sales-growth point of view, untapped domestic markets are generally better opportunities than unknown overseas markets that are much farther removed from your existing base of business experience. If, on the other hand, you are already broadly serving the domestic market, or if the remaining unserved domestic areas are particularly competitive, it may be time to explore export options.

Your first task in evaluating export potential is to develop a general understanding of demand, pricing and distribution in the target markets. What advantages accrue to local competitors? Which exporters are doing well there? Can you make a fair return? What additional levels of cost, investment and time will be required? Do you have the cash-flow flexibility to support such an endeavor? Unless you have highly reliable foreign subcontractors or partners for most key areas of the business, you will need to start off very slowly, first building your own base of expertise and knowledge before making major commitments to a new market. If you do have reliable foreign subcontractors or partners, their full costs need to be incorporated into all forecasts, and working arrangements must be explicitly defined in clear agreements.

Unless you have highly reliable foreign subcontractors or partners for most key areas of the business, you will need to start off very slowly, first building your own base of expertise and knowledge before making major commitments to a new market.

Inventory and receivables are two cash drivers that are almost inevitably different in export environments, compared with domestic business. Transportation, customs and paperwork delays will probably add significantly to inventory days associated with the export portion of your business. Accounts receivable are usually best handled through a letter-of-credit arrangement available through larger banks and some medium-size ones. Be sure to get these arrangements in place before booking that first overseas sale. Since letters of credit generally count against your line of credit, be sure your banking relationships and credit capacity are adequate before embarking on your export strategy.

In many cases, the export portion of your business will have operating and financial characteristics so different from your past experience that it will be almost like entering a different industry. This is not necessarily a brick wall, but it does raise the question, how different is too different? There is no easy answer, of course, but generally this question needs to be evaluated in terms of what you bring to the table. What skills, relationships, competencies or knowledge bases do you already have that will help you maintain and enhance your cash drivers in the new market? If you don't already have some significant part of what it will take, perhaps your long-term growth strategy needs to develop along an avenue other than export.

Ultimately, the firms that most completely master the issues of strategic integration at the cash-driver level, whether from domestic or export business, will maximize shareholder value. It is appropriate that we turn next to the assessment of such value in cash-flow terms.

Risk, Return & Valuing Cash Flows

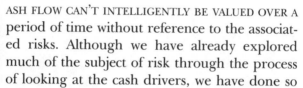ASH FLOW CAN'T INTELLIGENTLY BE VALUED OVER A period of time without reference to the associated risks. Although we have already explored much of the subject of risk through the process of looking at the cash drivers, we have done so specifically only in the sense of operating risk. There is another dimension of risk, that of financial risk to the business's financial stakeholders. These are the firm's lenders and owners, and the risk to them is erosion in the market value of the debt and equity they hold.

Debt & Equity Values

The market value of debt and equity taken together make up the earnings value, or going-concern value, of the firm's assets. On the balance sheet, we measure those assets at either cost or market value, whichever is lower, meaning simply that we record them at what we paid for them unless there has been a clear and measurable loss in value, in which case we write them down as an extraordinary loss. This lower-of-cost-or-market practice is part of the body of generally accepted accounting principles and is related to accounting's conservatism principle. Most typically, though, recording balance-sheet values at the lower of cost or market really means cost, unless there is some clear and compelling evidence of a need to write down, or devalue, one or more assets.

The real value of the firm is rarely, if ever, based on book value, that is, the accounting value of the assets. Rather, it is based on the cash-earnings stream those assets are likely to produce. The higher the expected cash-earnings stream, the higher the market value. Value is also enhanced by growth in that cash-earnings stream. The higher the growth rate, the higher the market value. And, finally, there is the issue of reliability. The more stable the pattern of the cash-earnings stream, the more it is valued. Good cash earnings, then, with high growth and consistency, make market value. The reverse is also true. Lower and less-certain streams, with slow or no growth, reduce market value by adding to risk. The marketplace treats risk as a cost and, in effect, deducts that cost from what might otherwise be the standard market value of a a firm with average earnings, average growth, average stability and average risk. How this risk is evaluated is quite different for lenders and for equity owners, that is, shareholders.

The real value of the firm is rarely, if ever, based on book value, that is, the accounting value of the assets. Rather, it is based on the cash-earnings stream those assets are likely to produce.

In their evaluation of risk and its associated costs, bankers are increasingly separating credit decisions from business decisions. The credit decision revolves around whether to make a particular loan. The business decision begins after a positive credit decision is made. It centers on the loan's terms, especially interest rate, along with collateral and guarantees. For the lender, additional risk is compensated for by a combination of higher interest rate and greater security. If the banker can quantify the fact that company A has a loan default probability of 2% and company B a default probability of 5%, then some calculable combination of fees, higher interest rate and more collateral can offset the risk differential. The enhancement of collateral most commonly takes the form of a legally documented interest in either company B's assets or its owners' guarantees. In sophisticated banking systems, additional factors in pricing loans are increasingly being considered so that the overall profitability of a firm's relationship with the bank can be readily and automatically figured.

It is likely that virtually all larger banks will eventually try to price loans based on the profitability of the overall relationship as expressed in terms of the bank's desired return on equity. This pricing strategy will explicitly consider all costs, including cost of risk. It will also include all revenues, including indirect revenue such as the value of noninterest-bearing deposit balances. The key point is that risk has a cost associated with it, and the financial community is rapidly improving its use of technology to estimate that cost. Computers and communication technology, and most especially the Internet, are already beginning to radically accelerate the rate of change in risk analysis and marketing practices in commercial lending. This will develop even more rapidly over the next few years—probably even faster than we have seen recently on the consumer side of financial services.

It is likely that virtually all larger banks will eventually try to price loans based on the profitability of the overall relationship as expressed in terms of the bank's desired return on equity. This pricing strategy will explicitly consider all costs, including cost of risk.

For shareholders, the cost of risk, although just as real as it is for lenders, is quite different in nature. It is also calculated in a somewhat less precise fashion and shaped by different dynamics of risk and reward. Whether or not a loan is explicitly collateralized or guaranteed, the lender always has the superior claim on the assets of the firm over the equity holder. In addition, because the market value of equity is what's left after all debts are satisfied, equity carries greater risk than debt. This differing nature of risk between debt holders and equity holders also implies a different reward structure. While the risk of loss is lower for lenders, the lender doesn't participate in the additional market value created by an enhanced cash-earnings stream. That enhancement of value goes almost exclusively to equity holders in exchange for the higher risk that they bear.

If a particular debt is relatively long-term in nature, and if the firm's cash-earnings stream is significantly enhanced in some way, then such an implied lessening of risk may accrue a bit of additional market value for the debt holder. This presumes that the debt can be traded in an organized venue such as a rated bond market. So, for example, if a low-rated long-term bond has its rating upgraded, it comes to be seen as less risky, and some of the risk premium will go out of the yield expected by the market. Since the bond's face amount and stated interest rate are generally fixed, the result will be an increase in the market value of the bond.

> **If a particular debt is relatively long term in nature, and if the firm's cash-earnings stream is significantly enhanced in some way, then such an implied lessening of risk may accrue a bit of additional market value for the debt holder.**

Chapter 7 explained that earnings are valued in three layers: their current level, their growth rate and their pattern of stability. Since these measures are based on expectations over a relatively long term, it is much more difficult to estimate the market value of equity than to estimate the value of debt. With the exception of bonds and mortgages, debt is almost always viewed on a much shorter time horizon than equity. Repayment of debt is also significantly more certain than is growth, or even recapture, of equity investment. This is due to the inherently different levels of risk involved. Finally, equity is riskier than debt because we value the cash-earnings streams in perpetuity rather than in the limited duration of particular debt agreements. For example, forecasting the ability of a firm to pay off a five year equipment loan is a lot easier than estimating a cash-earnings stream into perpetuity because we are usually valuing an entity, the corporation, which has no arbitrary limit to its life. Further, the corporation, according to generally accepted accounting principles, is valued as a going concern, with no thought of ever winding down or intentionally liquidating. Since company value is the sum of the market value of debt and the market value of equity, the point here is simply to understand that different levels of risk, uncertainty and duration have to be considered as debt and equity are separately evaluated.

The Market's Move to Using Cash Flow to Evaluate a Business

As I've already observed, bankers are generally the ones with the clearest view and sharpest focus on cash flow for one very simple reason: The loan is made in cash, and the bank wants to be repaid in cash. In valuing debt, we value it in cash, not earnings. Traditionally, though, equities have been valued in earnings rather than cash, although there is a shift under way in that practice. For all the analytical and historical reasons already cited, cash flow is ultimately more central to valuation than earnings.

There is one additional major reason for the shift away from earnings, and toward cash flow, for valuation purposes. That is to sidestep the impact of tricky accounting techniques so often used in mergers and acquisitions. The increased emphasis on cash flow on the part of the accounting and investing community is further testimony to the logic of specifically rooting valuation in cash flow and not in earnings. It can be argued as well that the traditional earnings focus of the past was always just a surrogate for estimating cash flow over the longer term.

How to Value Cash Flows Through Discounting

To evaluate a business on the basis of cash flow, we look at the pattern of cash flows a company may be expected to generate in the future, then calculate the compound value of those cash flows backward to get today's value. In its essence, this *discounted cash flow* (DCF) is the reverse of compound interest. With compound interest, we calculate the future value of a series of investments or deposits made at certain rates and at particular points in time. The simplest example of this future-value calculation would be a savings account where x dollars are deposited today at y interest rate and a dollars are deposited next month or year at b interest rate. We then compute what the account balance will be at some future time.

One obviously important variable in DCF is the discount rate used. A 5% rate on a savings account will compound to a bigger balance in the future than a 3% rate. With DCF analysis, though, backward compounding, or discounting, will yield a lower present value as the rate used goes higher. It is clearly in the owner's interests to minimize the discount rate. This is the opposite of investing, where we want the values to go up by maximizing the rate of return.

The rate at which the discounting of future cash flows is done is called the *weighted average cost of capital* (WACC) and is made up of two prime components; the debt portion and the equity portion.

The rate at which the discounting of future cash flows is done is called the *weighted average cost of capital* (WACC) and is made up of two prime components; the debt portion and the equity portion. To get the debt portion, first calculate the after-tax cost of debt (because interest is tax-deductible) and weight it by its share of total capital. For example, if the average interest rate on all debt is 10%, debt makes up 30% of total capital, and the marginal income-tax rate is 40%, then the debt portion of the WACC is: 0.10 x 0.30 x 0.40 = 1.2%

Then calculate the equity-cost portion of WACC and weight it in proportion to total capital. Assume that a generally good market estimate for cost of equity in medium-size, closely held firms can be approximated by multiplying average interest rate on debt by 2 to 2.5. Let's use the midpoint of 2.25.

The solution is 2.25 x 0.10 (average interest rate on debt) x 0.7 (proportion of equity in total capital) = 15.75%. This is the equity portion of WACC. Add it to the debt portion above (1.2%) for a total WACC of 16.95% This is the rate to use to discount future cash flows back to the present value of the company.

To do this accurately, though, you need to calculate a WACC for each year in which you will make an explicit cash-flow forecast, then use those individual rates to discount back the cash flows.

Pricing for Basic Risk

It is almost impossible to forecast with much confidence beyond five to seven years. For that reason it is probably best to do an explicit cash-flow forecast for no more than that same five to seven years, then assume that the subsequent years' results and WACC will continue in perpetuity. Implicit within this assumption are that sales growth will exactly equal inflation from that last year onward and that all of the other cash drivers will remain constant. The remaining task at this point is to set values for the interest rate on debt and the rate of return the market would expect on equity for the valuation periods. To figure interest rate on debt, first estimate prime rate, then add in whatever risk premium you think the bank is likely to require. This would be the premium for risk beyond the norm, unless that risk is offset to any degree by collateral or guarantees. For average risk in smaller companies having no specific collateral or guarantees, two to three points over prime is probably a realistic starting point. Think for a moment in terms of a simple and somewhat arbitrary model of what goes into the prime lending rate in general terms as a percentage of assets:

Underlying true time value of money, in the sense of deferred gratification	1.5%
Inflation expected in the time period	2.0
Average loan loss-rate	2.0
Direct noninterest expense (loan officers, branches, computers etc.)	0.75
Administrative costs	0.75
Profit	1.0

(These assumptions and approximations of the components of interest rates all generally prevail in the marketplace. They are seldom discussed systemically but do in fact explain interest-rate structures fairly well.)

Add these factors up, and you get to a prime rate of 8%. If higher levels of perceived risk or higher proportional levels of operating or administrative costs are encountered, as is often the case with smaller firms, then two to three points over prime is generally appropriate, especially for longer-term loans. Accordingly, you might use 9.75% for revolving credit, 10.25% for terms up to three years and 11% beyond three years.

Equity holders, because of their significantly higher level of risk, will ordinarily require a rate of return of at least two to two and a half times that of debt holders, depending on perceived financial and business risk. The financial risk is mostly a function of leverage, which really speaks to the residual value for stockholders after all creditors are satisfied. The lower the leverage, the more residual value there is for equity holders. The business risk reflects the probability that the company may not appropriately manage the cash drivers over the longer haul.

In almost every case, the true return actually available to equity holders is augmented beyond the nominal level of two to two and a half times the debt holder's return. This augmentation comes via some tax advantages not available to debt holders. Longer-term capital gains get preferential tax rates; taxation on gains can be postponed at least until sale; and certain qualifying transactions involving the exchange rather than outright sale of stock may be tax-deferred.

The stockholder's expectation of two to two and one half times the debt holder's return translates to a 20% to 25% return for the stockholder plus some tax advantages. It is also the equivalent of paying four to five times current cash flow for the stock, before factoring in the effect of any tax advantage. If, however, there is the expectation of rapid growth in the cash flow of the firm, then the multiple of current cash flow one will pay rises even further. If the company also has a record of consistently delivering on cash-earnings expectations, there is a market premium, a slightly higher multiple as well. Investors will always pay more for growth and predictability, while they discount for stagnation or surprises.

Summarizing the Basic Steps of the Mechanics of the Valuation Process

Let's use a mathematical example to summarize the basic steps of the mechanics of the valuation process. We'll assume our company stands with $1,000,000 in debt (interest-bearing only—not payables, accrued expenses, etc.), $2,000,000. in stock and retained earnings, and $2,598,803 in total liabilities.

1. CALCULATE AFTER-TAX WEIGHTED AVERAGE COST OF CAPITAL (WACC).
Debt portion:
10% interest rate on 0.33 of capital at 0.34 tax rate = 0.10 (interest rate) x 0.33 (proportion in capital structure) x 1– 0.34 (tax rate because interest is deductible) = 0.02178

PLUS:
Stock and retained earnings portion:
0.67 of total capital structure x 2.25 (midpoint in our 2- to- 2.5 ratio of market expectation of equity return as multiple of interest rate) x 10% debt (interest rate) = 0.15075

WACC = 0.02178 + 0.15075 = 0.17253–round to 17.25%

2. FORECAST YOUR CASH FLOW FOR THE NEXT FIVE YEARS.
Define cash flow as:
Cash after operations x 1 – 0.34 (tax rate) – depreciation.
(This is assumed to be equal to capital spending, so that cash after operations from the cash-flow statement comes before any payment to debt or equity holders. Cash after operations is used because we are trying to find the value of cash flows available to debt and equity holders. If we use a cash-flow figure after interest or principal or dividends, we no longer have a pure "available to debt and equity holders value" because we would already have paid out at least some of that value.)

Projected cash flow is:
   Year 1 $1,000,000
   Year 2 $1,100,000
   Year 3 $1,210,000
   Year 4 $1,331,000
   Year 5 $1,464,100

3. DETERMINE TODAY'S MARKET VALUE OF THE COMPANY'S CASH FLOWS OVER THE NEXT FIVE YEARS.
Discount the five-year cash flows back to present value using a constant WACC.
(A simplifying assumption here and in the next step is that there is no change in WACC from year 1 because of a stable

economy, low inflation and steady growth sustainable with the same basic cash-driver values and unchanging leverage factor. If these assumptions are not valid, a WACC would need to be calculated for each year.)

The cash flow for each of the five years is discounted back—year 1 cash flow is discounted back one year, year 2 cash flow is discounted back two years, etc. The results are added together.

The general formula for each year is:

Present value = cash-flow amount X $(1+0.1725)^n$.

Recall that .1725 is the WACC from Step 1 above, and n is the number of years.

$1,000,000 1 yr. @ .1725 = $852,878
$1,100,000 2 yrs. @ .1725 = $800,142
$1,210,000 3 yrs. @ .1725 = $750,666
$1,331,000 4 yrs. @ .1725 = $704,250
$1,464,100 5 yrs. @ .1725 = $660,703

Add present values of first five years' cash flows to estimate of today's market value of the company's cash flows over the next five years:= $3,768,639.

4. TAKE THE VALUE OF THE FIFTH YEAR'S CASH FLOW AS A PERPETUAL ANNUITY FROM THE SIXTH YEAR FORWARD, THEN DISCOUNT THAT VALUE FIVE YEARS BACK.

(We are assuming here that cash-flow growth in year 6 and beyond is not really forecastable, so it is presumed to grow equal to inflation, that is, there is no real growth from that point forward.)

$1,464,100 is the fifth-year cash flow assumed to be a perpetual annuity and therefore having a present value equal to the annuity amount divided by the discount rate (cash flow ÷ discount rate: in this case, $1,464,100 ÷ 0.1725) = $8,487,536. But the annuity doesn't start until the end of the fifth year, meaning that we need to further discount the $8,487,536 back five years according to the formula:

Present value = $8,487,536 ÷ (1+.1725)^5 = $3,830,164

5. ADD THE RESULT OF STEPS 3 AND 4, THEN SUBTRACT TOTAL LIABILITIES TO GET THE NET VALUE OF EQUITY

$3,768,639 (present value of first five years cash flow)
+ $3,830,164 (present value of cash flow from year 6 to forever)
$7,598,803 (gross value of equity)
− $2,598,803 (total liabilities)
$5,000,000 (net value of equity)

Note that in Step 1 book value of equity was only $2,000,000. The cumulative performance of management in managing the cash drivers has therefore created an additional $3,000,000 in market value. Hey, let's give them some performance-based options and see what happens!

You may have noted through all these discussions that there is no adjustment for volatility of cash flow. The simplifying assumption here is that cash-flow growth is relatively even. If it is even and predictable, there will be a premium; if it's erratic, a discount.

Improvement in any of the three areas—that is, current cash flow, growth rate of cash flow or predictability of cash flow—will add to the firm's market value. Maximizing each of those value categories requires that you work those cash drivers strategically.

What's Next?

HE GOAL OF THIS BOOK HAS BEEN TO SENSITIZE you to cash-flow thinking through the use of the seven cash drivers. At this point you should have a fairly good grasp of how cash—actual cash, rather than accrual-based accounting value—fuels an enterprise, and how cash flow can be shaped to meet different business needs.

Management's most basic job is to ensure that a company does not run out of fuel. Beyond that basic task, every other significant management effort has to be undertaken with an awareness of the impact on the fuel gauge, the cash-flow statement. In this model, the cash drivers are the basic internal fuel controls.

If you speed up by growing sales faster, you will burn your fuel faster. Letting the accounts-receivable days drift upward is like siphoning off fuel from your car to help another driver who promises to give it back. If accounts-payable days increase, you have just the reverse: Suppliers are allowing you to siphon fuel off from them, which, of course, you promise to give back sometime. If inventory days start rising, it's like taking fuel out of your tank and storing it in 55-gallon drums up north in the woods behind your vacation place. The fuel is still yours, but it's not readily and economically usable to top off your tank for tomorrow's long road trip.

Gross margins can be thought of as the basic efficiency measure of the business's engine. And gross margin's flip side, the cost-of-goods-sold percentage, tells you the rate of fuel burned per horsepower per hour. Then there is SG&A, the operating-cost ratio. It represents the efficiency of all the rest of the vehicle—transmission, aerodynamics, exhaust system, cooling system—and their overall effect on gas mileage. Capex is your investment in any of the vehicle's components for purposes of replacement and improvement. Or perhaps Capex is simply expansion of your fleet as your family grows, with those teenagers looking forward to their learner's permits and vehicles of their own.

The most basic and immediate step you can take now is to use your heightened cash-flow consciousness to become a generally better manager or a more broadly contributing individual employee.

Here now are several directions in which you might want to consider moving. The most basic and immediate is that you use your heightened cash-flow consciousness to become a generally better manager or a more broadly contributing individual employee. The next step up would be to be get a copy of your company's cash-flow statement and review it as background to every significant issue and decision in your job. At level three, you might use this book as the subject of a discussion group among your peers and subordinates, with a view toward relating your current business issues to your company's cash-flow statement. Next, you may want to engage a qualified consultant to do a historic and projected cash-driver analysis in dialogue with your key players, and elicit their perspectives on the core issues of your operation. Finally, there is the option of developing a complete analysis of your particular situation into a case study for seminar-style presentation throughout the organization, so that every employee appreciates the benefits of enhancing cashflowability.

Wherever you go, with whatever level of new insight this book has helped you to develop, may your cash flow always be positive!

Index

A

Accounting
accrual-based, 9-10, 11, 24
balance sheets, 33, 34-37, 40, 42-47,
51, 70-72, 81, 156-157, 172-174,
176, 177, 195-196
cash-based, 9-10
equation, 34-36
income statements, 33, 36-38, 42-47,
49, 51, 54-55, 81, 156, 172-174
matching principle, 9-10, 55
Accounts payable
accrued expense and, 41, 148-149
aging and, 148
balance sheet and, 36
description, 15, 22
prioritizing and policing payables,
148-150, 207
suppliers and inventory, 145-147
tax issues, 148
up-front negotiation principle,
146-147
Accounts receivable
aging reports, 122-123
balance sheet and, 36
cash flow and, 126-127
construction, defense and
aerospace industries and, 126
credit-check function, 126-127
days receivable, 75, 121-122, 207
description, 15, 22, 121
distribution-channel strategy,
124-125
exporting and, 124-125, 192
factoring, 127-129
industry norms, 125-127
invoices and, 123
marketing and, 124-125
on-time focus for customers, 122-123
Accrual-based accounting, 9-10, 11,
24. *See also* Double-entry system
of accounting

Acquisitions. *See* Mergers and
acquisitions
Activity ratios, 65-66
Activity-based costing (ABC) systems,
108-110
Airlines
cash drivers and, 23
perishability principle, 113
American Institute of CPAs (AICPA),
55, 179
Amgen, Inc., 124-125
"As though cash" assumption, 49-50,
176-177
Asset conversion, 19
Asset-efficiency measures
accounts payable and, 66
accounts receivable and, 65-66
activity ratios, 65-66
assets divided by sales, 67
cash balances, 66-67
contracting out, 68-69
inventory and, 65-66
leasing an asset, 67
management time and, 68
return on assets, 67

B

Balance sheets
balance sheet/income statement
connection, 36-37, 42
cash-driver shaping and, 172-174,
176, 177
cash-flow statements and, 49, 51
common sizing, 45-46
current ratio data and, 71-72
deferred income taxes payable,
156-157
description, 33
inventory and, 40
leasing and, 157
liquidity and, 70